For years I'd been driven to get high heroes treaded, and it was where the p————, —— ————————— ———— ———— experiences, half a mile above the floor of the earth, led to the greatest revelations, highs, visions, and clarity of mind.

Durango was so close to the desert, and thus the desert became all that mattered to me in climbing. Just like wall climbing, the desert is a fantastic rabbit hole to go down. I started to view the desert in a multitude of ways. As a home. As a canvas to paint my art. My own field of dreams where I could return to a childlike state of being, with the repose of an adult. A place where I could progress my vision of what it meant to be an American climber.

"Luke Mehall is one of the few adventure writers out who handle the tricky first person voice as if it were made for him."

John Long, climbing legend and Senior Contributing Editor,
Rock and Ice

"Who's more in tune with the ethos of the dirtbag—and more able to write passionately and honestly about it—than Luke Mehall? I think no one."

Brendan Leonard, of Semi-Rad.com, author of *60 Meters to Anywhere*

"In his third and most intimate book, Luke Mehall brings the abstract realm of personal transformation back down to earth. With sparse, masterful prose that reads like an old friend telling stories over a beer, American Climber weaves the complex and ever-changing personalities of rock climbing, our country, and Mehall himself into one seamless story."

Georgie Abel, climber/writer/poet

"American Climber isn't just about climbing; it is a strong and well-told story about climbing out of the gray cave of existential depression that infects so many young people today, an always-honest account of finding meaning in his life not through disposable McJobs or the standard-issue American dream, but through self-medicating on nature and nature's challenges, where the true highs of life and living are hard-earned doing strange things in strange places with a band of brothers and sisters equally disaffected but spirited. I've previously said that Mehall could be the Kerouac of his generation; with American Climber, he's there.'

George Sibley, author of *Dragons in Paradise* **and** *Water Wranglers,* **and longtime contributor to the** *Mountain Gazette*

American Climber

by Luke Mehall

Cover design by Mallory Logan (www.go-roshambo.com)

Cover photo of the author climbing Superette Crack in Indian Creek by Nick Chambers

Chief Editor: Lindsey Nelson (www.exactedits.com)

Excerpts of this book have been previously published in *The Climbing Zine, Rock and Ice*, and *the Alpinist*. Earlier versions of a couple chapters were also published in *The Great American Dirtbags* and *Climbing Out of Bed*.

For my mom, dad, and brother, Clint. You taught me the greatest lesson I've learned thus far in life: the meaning of unconditional love.

I spent a little time on the mountain

Spent a little time on the hill

Things went down we don't understand

But I think in time we will

—Grateful Dead, "New Speedway Boogie"

Author's note:

When I was a child, I had a severe case of what doctors call attention deficit hyperactivity disorder (ADHD or ADD). I was treated with medicine, my parents tried to remove sugar from my diet, and, in general, I was an angsty spirit who got into trouble and fights. I was also obsessed with sports; the hours spent playing basketball in my front driveway and pretending I was a hero are some of my most vivid memories as a kid growing up in the Midwest.

I hope that someday ADD will be renamed, because there's another side to it, a most beautiful, creative, mind-expanding side. I can only speak for myself, but, once I found something I loved in the intellectual arena, I discovered I could focus for hours at a time, a deep, profound, meditative focus. It took me three colleges and many, many courses to find my passion, but there it was, in the written word.

I found focus in climbing as well. Climbing allowed the same escape as the concrete driveway, except the stakes were much more than imaginary games—they were life and death. Thus, a new focus had to be found, and, much more importantly, I had to learn how to be brave. These lessons happened on rocks across the United States, starting with the sweaty gray sandstone of Southern Illinois, to the unforgiving granite of the Gunnison Valley, Colorado, and eventually stretching to the West Coast, to California and the rock climbing Promised Land that we call Yosemite. And there was much in between.

What lies in between is the ether, and a sort of holding on to the past, while trying to let it be the past, and still hoping your best days are in front of you. One moment, you're packing a pickup truck, heading west with barely a couple hundred bucks that is supposed to last for the entire trip, and, the next moment, you've got a wife and baby in tow, and you're signing for a mortgage. I have managed to avoid the major commitments of adulthood thus far; perhaps that is why I have the leisure time to compose these words.

And a few words on why I write these stories—I have to. I've made the decision as a writer to make it on my own. Several years ago, I left behind a better paying writing job, with benefits, to pursue this path of writing books, all the while holding down a "day job" to pay the bills. In the last two years, I've seen my work go to print, and now, with two books of short stories under my belt, I'm finally ready for this leap into a memoir.

These days, at thirty-seven years old, I love climbing more than I ever have. And the writing flows well; I am not the type of writer who says you have to write every day—I am the type of artist that says if the writing isn't happening that day, go do what you love, if you can. Go breathe the fresh air and clear the mind; go dream and keep it fresh.

Even if I knew only a few people would read it, I would still write this book. The fact that I know many more than a handful will read it feels like the greatest blessing of my life—that my passion and my work can overlap so heavily. I thank you for that!

Word.

Luke Mehall

Durango, Colorado

Chapter 1

The beauty is in the simplicity.

A hunger fed by nature, a modern way of experiencing nature. We were driven out there for different reasons—some of us introduced to rock climbing at a young age, in a responsible manner. For others, including myself, it was trial by fire.

And it was fire from a nearby controlled burn that created the sunset that evening as we stood atop El Capitan in Yosemite. Dave and I were celebrating two things: one that we had climbed El Cap, and, equally as important, that we found two packages of tuna in our haul bag, a bag we'd been living out of for the last four days as we inched up the rock.

El Capitan was our Mount Everest, our Mount Analogue, the pinnacle we had to face if we wanted to continue to live as climbers, and to grow as human beings. This was my third attempt; the three-thousand-foot golden-granite monolith had haunted and inspired my existence since I first laid eyes on it over a decade ago.

It became a singular goal I had in the back of my mind and an easy reference when people would ask me what my life goal in climbing was. It is a rock easier to capture in prose than a photograph, more reasonable to ponder over a week than a moment, worthy of a book rather than a paragraph. Technology, coupled with bravery, has allowed human beings to climb it, and, in turn, climbing it offered an alternative viewpoint of life itself, much like the essence of climbing.

I danced and screamed when we found that tuna. Dave rolled it up into a burrito and it was the most delicious meal my mouth had ever tasted. And that sunset, it was delicious as well.

I felt so connected to that sunset. It was fire red, so surreal it made life seem like the ending of an epic movie, and we took it in slowly. Below us was three thousand feet of air, and above us was only sky. In that sunset was everything: our hopes and dreams, our past and our future, our moment in time. We'd accomplished our greatest rock climbing feat, the alluring and intimidating face that is a symbol of Yosemite, and America.

And then when the sunset was over, so was our high, at least for then. The beauty of that red faded, and then smoke from the fire filled the air. It was a restless night of sleep atop The Captain, and, in the morning, we descended from the mountain of our dreams.

Chapter 2

It all began, my climbing life, near the end of my time in the flatlands when I was battling some serious mental illness that nearly killed me. I won't bother talking about that too much; many of us have our epic of sadness, our tragedy, real or imagined, and I hit mine at twenty years old, right in the heartland of America.

My sadness began with happiness—a child of sport, a kid who read his first words in the sports page of the local newspaper, and lived a life of fantasy in his mind. I was obsessed with basketball, baseball, and football. Watched all the games, collected baseball cards, and spent hours in the front driveway, shooting hoops; with each passing hour playing ball with my friends, I became more lost in play, into my happy place. I was watched over by two loving parents, who provided for me and cared for me; simple middle-class Midwesterners, my dad was an accountant, and my mom was a teacher.

I've blocked out the boring parts of my childhood. I have a hard time remembering the names of my teachers and classmates, perhaps a symptom of ADD, but I can vividly remember the basketball court outside of my parents' house. A simple concrete driveway with a hoop, and that was where I would spend many hours, practicing shooting, playing pickup games, and, most importantly, living out the fantasy that I was the star in the final game, and I had to make the shot for our team to win.

The highlight of my basketball career came before my freshman year of high school when my parents sent me to Michael Jordan basketball camp. The camp was just two blocks from my grandmother's house in the suburbs of Chicago. We got daily talks from Mr. Jordan himself, and I watched wide-eyed as my hero dropped his knowledge to us. It was probably the best week of my childhood; I found an intense focus and even made the All-Star team at the camp. In reality, I wasn't that good; I was just better than the other suburban kids who had the money to go to the camp. I knew there were many kids back home who were better than me, but their parents couldn't afford to send them to the camp.

My childhood sports fantasies died shortly after, as I approached sixteen. I was cut from tryouts for the basketball team my freshmen year of high school, and, instead of crying like I would have in junior high, I simply stopped trying.

Then it was cars. Ford Mustangs became my obsession. I worked hard at my restaurant job and saved my pennies. And, finally, I earned enough money to buy a real Mustang, a 5.0L V8, the Fastest Car In My High School. How did I know? Anyone who thought they had a contender would square up with me on some country roads and drag race alongside the cornfields. I never lost.

This was just the beginning of my taste for illegal behavior. Perhaps it's an American thing. Freedom. My friends and I drove our fast cars around and found liquor and easy women. Dangerous things at any age. And then marijuana. Probably the least dangerous of those three. And then psychedelics, powerful and dangerous. The best. Or the worst. Depending on the vibes.

I had crashed more than one car by the time I was a senior in high school. The fast Mustang was the last to crash, but it was a reality check. I didn't have a car for a while, and then I got the cheapest car possible, an old Honda, barely running, with the bumpers falling off.

I was going through phases, like any teenager will. Was I the sports guy, or the car guy? Clearly I was skilled at neither. And then, shortly after that first hit of weed, some new vibrations were in the air. Jerry Garcia and The Grateful Dead. I started listening to The Dead the week Garcia died. At first it was just one song that entranced me, then many. And, as my sports fantasies were dying, and I didn't know what my passion was, I decided that I would become a hippie.

I was as poorly suited to become a hippie as I was a sports guy. But I went there—I bought the Dead albums, traded bootlegs, started smoking weed every day, took mushrooms and LSD, and made new hippie friends. This all collided with my preppy-sports-car-guy image, and awkwardness was legendary. Growing up in America.

God knows what my parents thought of me in those days. My

parents are simple Midwestern Catholics. The best of that in every way. They were simple, and I was complex. Confused. Lost. Just trying to find something real in the world.

There were nice side effects to the confusion and awkwardness. First, when I started smoking pot all the time and was in a trance with The Dead, I lost my desire to fight. All my life I'd been a fighter. From grade school through high school, I rarely backed down from an argument, resulting in more than one suspension, and more than one black eye that I'd lie about to my parents.

And then there was Kerouac.

It's fucking cliché to write about Kerouac, so I will dance with him and his words. Hippies read Kerouac, especially *On the Road*, so I did too. I had an old paperback copy lent to me by a now-forgotten friend. Kerouac opened up The Road, even if it was a late 1950s highway. Once I learned that Kerouac and his buddy Neal Cassady, some of the original beatniks, were the predecessors to the hippies, that made me like them even more. Then I started to read Timothy Leary, the original American psychedelic academic hero, and things really got out there.

I don't think I was born to be *out there*. But I guess a lot of life is wasting time and figuring out who you are. Some Americans are born right into who they are, and, in some ways, I'm jealous of those people. Those who have one career and one wife and two kids and one truck and rarely leave the nest that is home and don't yearn and wander for more. Those who are happy with the simplicity that is Midwest America.

I had three genuine hippie friends I made in high school, and I looked to them as my spiritual, philosophical, and recreational guides. Two were roommates, they loaned me *On The Road, The Electric Kool-Aid Acid Test*, and the Timothy Leary books. One friend spent the summer in jail that year after high school, for something stupid, like weed. We wrote each other letters and poured our souls out to each other. The correspondence felt real, something that meant something to me and something to him. I'd always felt a calling to write—my mother was an English teacher. But until a man has experience, what can he really write about that anyone would want to read?

By the time my senior year at Bloomington High School had finished, things seemed to be going all right—on paper. I'd been accepted into college, my grades were okay, and I'd stopped getting into fistfights. But to maintain all of this, I had to take a lot of drugs. First, there were the cigarettes. I'd started innocently smoking a couple with my friends and then moved on to a pack a day. And I was taking Dexedrine, a stimulant used to treat ADD. I was also smoking pot, all the time. And drinking soda, a knock-off version of that green stuff that looks like nuclear waste. And alcohol, of course, the drink of the masses, the tonic that runs through the veins of nearly every single college student. My heart beat to the drum of substances.

The craziest part was that I probably seemed somewhat normal when I entered higher education. Sure, my hair was unruly, and I wore tie-dyed shirts, but what college campus doesn't have these sorts of characters running around? The first school I went to, Western Illinois University, was situated in a small town surrounded by cornfields, as much of Illinois is. It was a frat and sorority school, and, of course, I rejected getting involved in those sorts of things. But, essentially, the rituals of college are not that much different if you're in a frat, or not. Binge drinking, sleeping around, smoking weed, and a pack a day of cigarettes were a given. I did study, continuing to pump that cocktail of substances into my body.

The weirdest thing about this college was that one of the top majors was law enforcement. And these kids were the worst behaved. They abused drugs and alcohol more anyone else. Maybe they thought they were just getting it out of their systems, or maybe they were preparing to be corrupt big-city cops.

I survived that first year of college, but I didn't really like Western Illinois, so I decided to transfer down to Southern Illinois, where there were more hippies. A party school, a bad place to be lost.

That summer was a haze. Shit, ever since I embarked on such a strange yet very American cocktail of drugs, life was a haze. Something happened though; I tried rock climbing for the first time.

The rocks of the state are down in Southern Illinois. Gray sandstone outcroppings through rolling hills. One of my three hippie friends was Caleb, a wiry guy, who, like me, was a fiend for cigarettes and weed. He also had seen the Grateful Dead at that very last show in Soldier Field in Chicago. He was something of a veteran in a scene I wanted to be a part of.

So Caleb took me down to Jackson Falls, along with some of his buddies from the suburbs of Chicago, which was where he had moved to Bloomington from. Caleb had been talking climbing up since I first met him. I was interested in the trip because there would be beer and weed. We camped, and I hadn't camped since Family Camp, years before in Minnesota. We climbed. I didn't find it all that interesting. Some of the people on the trip were heroin addicts. They snuck away into their tents to put needles in their arms. We jumped off a thirty-foot cliff into a small pool of water. That was interesting but terrifying. We drove back into the normalcy of central Illinois.

I transferred to Southern Illinois University, down in Carbondale, where there were more hippies but the same general spirit of any large higher education institution. Plenty of frats and sororities. My tendencies toward drugs and alcohol were encouraged. A great sort of emptiness came over me, and I tried to fill it.

Chapter 3

America, I've given you all and now I'm nothing…

I can't stand my own mind…

I smoke marijuana every chance I get.

I sit at my house for days on end and stare at the roses in the closet.

—*Allen Ginsberg, "America"*

The most dangerous part of anyone's life is encountering risk and danger without any direction on how to dance with it. With sex, drugs, and rock 'n' roll there was something that captured my imagination, but I had no idea how to dance.

And I have no idea how I attracted a woman at that point in my life—awkward as I was. Perhaps she was on drugs. She was definitely on drugs. Cherise was a flower child, a hippie from the suburbs of Chicago who had the same taste for recreation that I did. She dressed in the type of homemade hippie clothes that many hippies wear and carried a scent of patchouli. I met her in the bar, and our relationship became one of weed and drunken hookups.

I operated from high to high—starting off in the morning with a cigarette, then popping Dexedrine to focus in school, getting high midday in my dorm room, and finishing most nights with alcohol. Then from time to time we'd take psychedelics, but my interest in those was waning because of bad trips. One time after eating some LSD, my equilibrium became disoriented, and I was unable to function. It lasted for hours. I put a glass on a table, and it appeared as though only half the glass was on the table—one of the most frightening experiences of my life; I thought it was never going to end. Another time, on mushrooms I had caught some bad vibes and started having a bad trip, and, with no mentor to help me through it, I hit the streets and walked alone. A fire hydrant sank deep into the earth and talked to me, saying something very sad. And then, on a flat sidewalk, I walked down, deep down, like an escalator moving down, and my heart sank into my stomach, and I wondered if I'd ever have a soul again.

I formed a hippie crew in Carbondale. We did hippie things, mostly smoking weed and going to late-night concerts. Cherise was my first real girlfriend, and I was happy to have a girlfriend. But could I take a girl like that home to Mom and Dad?

Geoff was a hippie friend from home. He seemed peaceful and mature enough—he had long locks of curly blond hair, and his apartment carried an air of hippie sophistication, with stones from across the West, a constant stream of burning incense mixed with Grateful Dead on the stereo, and always fine weed to be smoked. Geoff was a mentor for my hippie behavior, and, at our best moments, we escaped into the woods that surrounded Carbondale and had philosophical conversations about life. One time, driving back from a concert, we debated fate versus free will—like is everything all planned out by God, or do we, as humans, have control over our destinies? I figured, like a senior-level class, I could put that question off for the time being. "Hand me that pipe," I said.

Geoff once told me, "We need a new drug." I agreed that everything was getting old, and I was too young for things to get old. I guess that's why people try nasty drugs like heroin, cocaine, and crystal meth.

Sex was a mystery. I knew my body wanted it, but I had no idea how delicate the art of making love was or that making love and fucking were so different—like the sun and the moon. I just knew I had an urge deep in my body, and, like a frat boy trying to score on a Friday night, I put little thought into the consequences.

Cherise and I wrestled in the dorm room bed, driven to madness by alcohol. Growing up Catholic, I'd had little education on sex, outside of the classroom of public education, and really had no clue of how to make love. But, no one other than your lover can truly show you how to make love. So, we fucked, and maybe once there was magic, for a brief moment, but mostly it was drunken wrestling. We were desperate to achieve the act, but there was little of being in the moment, which is so important to love making.

And that was the style in which I participated in everything—a young man desperate to be a part of the world but with no education on how to do so. I kept following, and everything was about to fall apart.

Cherise lasted only a few months. My first heartbreak. She ended up cheating on me but probably only in the terms of my definition. She was my first girlfriend, but we never discussed the terms, or any sort of commitment to one another. She slept with another hippie during a weekend at a concert.

My college experience at Southern Illinois only lasted a semester. My grades were slipping, and, after discussing it with my parents, I decided to take a semester off. I moved back into their basement. And somewhere in the mix of this, a terrible depression came over me.

Looking back now, I can't really see where the storm came from, only that it must have been the culmination of depression, fear, anxiety, a lack of self esteem, and, of course, drugs and alcohol. But, the storm was a brewing.

I went back to the job I'd had in high school, bussing tables at a local sports bar and restaurant. I worked nights and would often not get out of my bed until early afternoon. My parents were frustrated with me and started charging me rent. I argued with them on everything from my marijuana use to my rejection of Catholicism. I continued to smoke a pack of cigarettes a day, smoke weed all day, and drink at night. Sometimes alone. I still occasionally popped the Dexedrine, if for no other reason than out of habit—perhaps to work harder and be more focused.

I don't know if it was Dexedrine, or nicotine, or marijuana that brought the disillusionment and the paranoia, but I began to think I was sick, and that I was going to die soon. That had to be the way out, I thought. Look at all the heroes from the sixties who died in their twenties. Surely, that must be my path, I thought.

I went to the doctor and got an STD test. That was what was wrong with me, I was sure of it. Cherise must have given me some disease—after all, her hygiene was beyond questionable, and she had cheated on me. I labored in pain and confusion while I waited for the tests to arrive back. At the beginning of my work shift, I would smoke cigarettes in the bathroom and just sit on the toilet and hide for the first hour when I was supposed to be cleaning. The tests came back, and I was clean. I celebrated by myself with cigarettes, and the high of being healthy lasted for a few hours. I was far from healthy.

A downward spiral continued. There were very little moments of happiness. My job was my savior, a chance for action, even if it was only a moment to escape the tyranny of my mind. Every insane, depressed person hopes for that, I imagine—to know that maybe one day life would be normal again, that not every day you will wake up and ask God why you were born and what your purpose is on planet earth.

One day, in the midst of all of this, Caleb took me climbing. This time we didn't have to drive four hours south to Carbondale; we simply crossed over to the other side of the tracks in Bloomington, to the climbing gym.

Chapter 4

It was the idea of a madman, surely—to clean out a series of abandoned grain silos, paste plastic climbing holds on the concrete walls and open it up as a climbing gym. At the time, my hometown climbing gym, Upper Limits, was billed as the largest in the world. And something about the simplicity and immediacy, the sport of it, drew me in, much more than climbing outside. It was a pill of Prozac, a shot of serotonin and endorphins into my hollow soul.

It all begins with the figure 8, the knot of eternity, a fitting beginning to something that can capture your life and make it whole, over and over, and be the center, that place you can go, as long as you are able to, to enter a moving meditation. That is now; this was then. It took me three days to master that knot, but, once I had it, I had it.

Caleb was a real climber. His brother and his uncle were climbers, and he'd climbed Devils Tower as a kid. He always spoke of going out West and had a general discontent for Bloomington. He was often quite negative, and so was I. We both seemed to think the world had little to offer us. Get him climbing, or talking about climbing, though, and a sparkle appeared in his eye, like the magic of Devils Tower came shining through some metaphysical channel into the moment.

So we climbed. The sixty-five-foot grain silos towered above me and were an immediate goal to reach the top, one of the more tangible goals I'd had in forever. We bouldered as well, crashing down to the pads in a cloud of chalk dust when we fell. We did pull-ups, and it felt good to exercise again. I hadn't had much of a routine since my front driveway basketball days.

Climbing was the only source of light in those dark ages. I immediately took my best friend Tim climbing there, and he liked it as much as I did. He was a wrestler in high school, and had a natural tendency for the balance and precarious physical situations that climbing puts you in.

Soon enough Caleb, Tim, and I were a trio of climbing fiends. We returned back to Southern Illinois for the outdoor experience, and I was planning to head back there for school in the fall. But, a dark cloud had moved into every cell of my being, and I never told anyone about it, which made it worse. I was possessed by doubt, fear, and delusion.

I should have confided in Tim. He was my best friend, and that's what best friends are for. He was so quiet and shy that in many situations I was our leader. When we would go to shows and sell beer and weed, I would do all the talking. I even got us out of a couple situations that could have landed us in jail, like the time we approached a road block in the middle of the cornfields of Indiana after a Phish show in Deer Creek. We were in a line of cars being stopped and searched, illegally I presumed, so I made up a speech to an officer about how we'd made a wrong turn, and we knew our rights, and we did not plan on being searched. Somehow that worked. Moments like that rushed us with adrenaline and made us feel alive. Tim and I were a duo: the slow and steady tortoise and the erratic, quick crow.

The idea that I was sick kept coming back. Maybe it was the cigarettes, or the Dexedrine, or the soda, or the alcohol, or maybe it was that I mixed all of that with marijuana—all the time. I began to research diseases online. I was fatigued, and I was depressed. I also could not stop thinking of Cherise. She appeared in my dreams, and I hoped to have her back someday, even if she had given me some sickness.

After searching and searching the Internet, I decided I had hepatitis. I went back to the doctor and got a test. I waited in pain and agony for the results to come back. Three days later, I called to check in. The office said I tested positive.

I didn't know what to do, but, in the back of my mind, there were two thoughts: suicide and running away to find Cherise. She was on the East Coast, I'd heard, on Phish tour. These were the days before cell phones, and I decided I would hit the road, in the middle of the night, and leave behind a trail of notes explaining my actions to my friends and family.

It doesn't even make sense now. But now I have the angle of repose in happiness and contentment. I have a foundation of good decision-making. At that point, I had been making bad decisions for years and was nearing the bottom of a shame spiral.

My selfish, insane departure had perfect timing. My parents were moving, and our house was in boxes. I felt so much despair and guilt, mixed with an excitement that I could be escaping the tyranny of my mind. I could not stand my mind. With my letters written, valuables sold for gas money, and a fresh pack of cigarettes, I left in the middle of the night in my little compact car, to find Cherise.

Chapter 5

In fourteen months I've only smiled once and I didn't do it consciously

Somebody's got to find your trail, I guess it must be up to me.

—*Bob Dylan, "Up To Me"*

It's painful to try to write this part of the story, as painful as it was to pack up everything and leave. In my mind, it was that or suicide. Something about me was consumed by demons, and I wanted to rid myself of them. Running away was the answer. I didn't know if I had it in me to kill myself; it was just a lingering thought that I wanted to be done with this existence.

It was pure survival mode. I slipped out of my parents' house at midnight, in a similar fashion I'd done in high school, escaping for a night of simple sinning, but now I was escaping forever from my childhood home.

The feeling of freedom is often false, like the freedom of too many drinks, where you feel like something is right, when it's really wrong. I was beyond right and wrong. I was hurting inside. My soul was dead.

But I felt that freedom as I drove twelve hours straight to the East Coast, where there were green rolling hills that welcomed me. Smoking cigarettes, drinking soda, and popping Dexedrine, I barely felt human, but I felt a release. I'd made an action. I didn't think about my parents, who were probably beyond distraught that their son had run away the very day they were moving into their new home. I didn't think about my friends, who probably felt worried and betrayed. I didn't think about work, where my shifts would have to be covered, and my coworkers were probably confused by my departure. I simply thought about finding Cherise.

I showed up at a Phish show in Virginia Beach, Virginia. I was certain that she was on Phish tour, from the word of mouth through my friends. Compared to now, 1999 might as well have been the Dark Ages. No one had a cell phone, at least not college kids or hippies scraping by for summer tour. E-mail was used, but not every day, every minute like it is now. It was all word of mouth.

Escape. At the Phish show, I felt a surge of adrenaline to have escaped. Maybe a similar surge to what an escaping prisoner might feel—sure to be caught, but free for a moment. At the concert, I enjoyed the escape of the music and felt like I was the only prisoner in a venue of tens of thousands of free people. I scoured every face for a glimpse of Cherise. So many women looked like her, every woman looked like her. Every hippie girl with dreadlocks and a sundress could be her. And how would she take this news? What did I expect from her after the arrival of the news? I was an insane man.

Then something happened. At the end of the show, while I was scanning anyone and everyone, I saw someone I knew. Bruno, a guy I went to school with at Southern Illinois. We embraced in a big hug, and I lied. I lied about why I was there and my plans for the future. It felt terrible to lie to a friend.

Bruno and I teamed up, and he took me to his place in Baltimore, close to where the next show would be. I faked happiness, like everything was normal, and I was just out catching some shows. I sold him my entire collection of CDs for gas money, and he asked me if I was sure. We went to two more shows in the area, and there was no sign of Cherise. I ran into some mutual friends, and they said she was on Widespread Panic tour, not Phish tour. Widespread was playing in Nebraska in two days. So, I drove to Nebraska.

Traversing back from the east to the Midwest, I was on the road, but there was nothing Kerouac about it. I guess maybe the sadness that is presented in his later work, the sadness that came later after the joy, was present. I was so profoundly sad I could not even cry a tear. I could not think about contacting my friends or family. The road was my home, and I didn't have a single connection to a person in the world. I had fits of anger where I would punch my steering wheel and dashboard. I ate fast food. All the time. And peanut butter and jelly sandwiches, my staple. My tape player was probably my best friend. I'd sold all my CDs for gas money, and I had seven tapes, which I played over and over, mixed with the sound of local radio stations when I could get them.

I wished and wished and wished my life could get back to normal. I'd go into a mall somewhere and see families and wished I could go back to being a child and start over. Everything made me sad.

I arrived at another concert. The scene was only a few hundred people versus thousands. No sign of Cherise in the audience. After the show, I picked up trash in the parking lot with some hope that karma could work off the monumental mistake that was my existence. I went to another show in St. Louis the next day. No sign of Cherise again. I noticed a couple people from my hometown, and I hid my face under my ball cap and hooded sweatshirt, for fear they had heard I'd ran away, and I would be discovered.

That night I was sitting in my car, in despair, no clue of what to do next, nowhere to go, nowhere to be, an adult runaway. Suddenly a police officer approached my car, "Get out of the car, and put your hands behind your head!" he said.

He had a gun drawn on me. I explained that this was my car. He explained there was a problem with robberies in this area. "You better get out of here, son," he told me. "For your own good."

I got a hotel room somewhere on the highway outside of St. Louis. I watched the sun come up that morning and could not appreciate the beauty. I noticed the beauty, the miracle that is the sun coming up every morning, but I was numb to it, dull, like beauty has to be a part of something bigger. There has to be happiness in your heart to feel beauty.

I did some research and found Cherise's parents' phone number. It was a call of desperation. Her mother picked up, and I explained what was happening. She was abrupt, "There is no way my daughter gave you hepatitis. She had a vaccine for that."

When I asked her where Cherise was, she said she did not know, but she had told her she was in Phoenix. What a sad world—neither of our parents knew where we were. They brought us into the world, with love, raised us, made sacrifices for two decades to try to give us a good life, and we were failures, distant, and absent.

I decided to drive west to Arizona on Interstate 70. For the first time as an adult, I crossed over through Colorado. I felt betrayed to see such beauty and magic and not have an ounce of enthusiasm for it. I arrived in Arizona a couple days later, haggard, over a week gone from home.

Chapter 6

I felt more lost in Phoenix than ever. At least at the concerts, there was an easy task of scanning every face to see if it was Cherise. And, there at the concerts, there was a small resemblance of what community is—on the road, and in the streets of the city, there was more of an empty void. I continued to hate myself, to punch my dashboard in anger, to smoke cigarettes slowly in the only form of suicide I was brave enough for.

I found a rest area to sleep at in my car, night after night. Sometimes I would fall asleep at the wheel, and be jolted awake as I drove off the road. That happened more than once. Death could have taken me, but I didn't have it in me to contemplate what form of suicide I would choose.

I did things alone. I played Frisbee golf. I went to bowling alleys alone during the day and smoked cigarettes. Goddamn, there's a whole layer of America that's perfectly suited for the suicidal, sad person, where you could live an entire lifetime in that state of being, and no one would even ask you if you were okay.

To find Cherise, I went to libraries and talked to librarians about how to find someone in the area. They had me looking through directories and searching on the Internet. It was a lost cause. I was not going to find Cherise.

One day, in my routine of wandering the city without purpose, I found myself in a park. There was a hill, a steep hill of mud and rocks, and I decided to climb up it. It was my first taste of exercise in three weeks. At one point, the angle steepened, and there was a big drop off, where a fall would mean certain injury—probably not death, but at least a broken arm, maybe a concussion if I hit my head right. Given the present moment, for the first time as a runaway, I clung to life. I completed the move, stood on top of the hill, and felt endorphins.

That afternoon, feeling alive, the sorrow of guilt from not contacting my parents weighed on my heart. Later in the day, I went over to the college campus and e-mailed them. The next day I returned again to the computer lab to find a message from them. It was stern. They communicated how disappointed they were in my actions, but they also expressed relief that I was alive, and they showed unconditional love. They would support me as I tried to climb out of my depression and as I was treated for hepatitis.

I left Phoenix and drove around the West. Both my parents and myself decided I should try to get back in college. Find some direction again. I was convinced I was sick and never going to have a lover again,

but I eventually came around to the idea that life has to go on.

I drove around Arizona, Utah, and into Colorado to find a college to go to. Everything was purely on a whim, how I felt when I was in a certain place. Nothing felt right, until I noticed a town called Gunnison, surrounded by green on the road map. The green was a million acres of National Forest, and the map indicated there was a liberal arts college there. I didn't know what a liberal arts college was. My negative mind told me I probably didn't belong there. I'd been in survival mode in academics my entire life, and, after two colleges, I didn't even have a clue as to what I would major in. The road led me there though, and I stopped in to the college to have a look.

Chapter 7

Gunnison quickly became a replacement home for my weary, tired vagabond existence. I made a campground by the Blue Mesa Reservoir my home and lived among the retired people living a similar yet, surely, more relaxed existence. I finally spoke to my parents on the phone, and they were, again, stern yet supportive. There was an underlying tone of unconditional love. I surely didn't love myself then, but at least I had some love. I spoke with Tim and Caleb, and they, indeed, felt betrayed, but, once that passed, we made plans to climb in Colorado. Caleb was moving out, and there was a feeling that Tim needed to get out as well. A great migration seemed to be in the air.

I began to form a routine, still deep in the throes of loneliness and hopelessness, but a routine nonetheless. My campsite was nine miles outside of town, and I paid five dollars a day to stay there— years later I would tell friends this, and they would make fun of me to no end because there is free camping just a mile outside of town at Hartman Rocks, a rolling landscape of sagebrush and granite domes and boulders, where the mountain lion roam, and, at night, when the stars fall, there's a feeling of no boundary between heaven and earth. I was not ready for such pleasures and joys anyways, so I moped around this paved campsite among retired seniors. In my heart, I believed I was older and more tired than all of them.

A depressed person needs little successes, tiny steps to try to regain that reason we're all here on this earth, to be happy and enjoy people and love. One day I rode nine miles on my bike into town. The bike had been on my car for the entire journey and had yet to be put to use. The ride felt monumental as I hacked up green phlegm from all my smoking.

I visited the doctor to find out how I would begin treating my hepatitis, and more tests revealed that I never had it. I tested positive because I had a vaccine for it. I was only sick in the mind and not in the body. It was a brief wave of relief, but I was still sick in the mind. Baby steps.

I felt incredible shame to have runaway for no real reason, and I never told a soul my real story. It was easy to hide in this little mountain town; every car's license plate seemed to be from another state. Plus there was a hippie vibe, and my appearance was more in the ordinary than anywhere I'd ever lived.

I applied to the college there, just a mere two weeks before classes would start, and I was accepted. The campus was beautiful, old red brick buildings and perfectly manicured green grass. There was a vibe that this was a place of true learning and discovery, not merely an education of transaction like the larger schools I went to in Illinois. Plus, there were no frats or sororities, and I liked that. To the south of campus was a small mountain—though all mountains seem large to a Midwesterner—that had a giant W, for Western State College. Later I would learn that ancient people lived atop the mountain some ten thousand years ago.

The mind of the flatlander cannot possibly comprehend the massive scale of wild lands, mountains, rocks, and wildlife that surround Gunnison. It's too much, too big, and, honestly, it meant little to me. I had to meet friends first.

My body was still in shock, my soul still desperate and tired, and I felt as lost as ever those first few weeks in Gunnison. At one moment, just after being accepted to Western State, I spoke with my brother and shared with him that I was going to move back home to Bloomington. I told him not to tell Mom and Dad.

But then, I just didn't move back. I don't really know why, perhaps some spirits or angels kept me there, the same ones that protected me as I fell asleep at the wheel and lived on the road. Maybe it was just luck. I was far from believing in positive spirits then, and, even now, as a believer in some greater higher power, I still don't have a firm opinion on why some people survive their epic of sadness, and why some people take their lives during that time. So many of us endure sadness, some meet their maker escaping the sadness, leaving others to be sad. Some of us live to tell the story and taste the sweet remedy that is redemption.

I moved into an apartment and made my first Gunnison friend, my upstairs neighbor, an older guy in his midthirties named John, who, like me, smoked weed and cigarettes. He was an East Coast guy who spoke tough but was a softie on the inside, and he shared with me whatever he had. I did the same. It was nice to have someone to talk to, though I didn't open up about all the pain I'd endured over the last six months. I didn't open up about it for years.

And, just six weeks after I ran away from everything I'd ever known, a new start officially began when fall courses commenced at my new place of study.

Chapter 8

Something's gotta change

Sounds of laughter and happiness turn my teardrops to rain

Been bearing this burden for too many of my days

Looks like breezes of autumn done finally blew my way

Like memories of yesterday

—Outkast, "13th Floor / Growing Old"

When a wildfire ravages through the forest, the devastation is not hard to see—the trees that remain standing are barren, the ground blackened, and it hardly resembles the healthy forest that once stood there. Give it some time though, and greenery starts to appear, flowers bloom again, and eventually young trees grow to replace the previous generation. If you could have looked into my soul, it was dark too, but Gunnison and the people who lived there put a new light and life into my being.

Just before classes started, I got a job as a dishwasher at a local restaurant with a small bar. The owner was a so-called recovering alcoholic, who had moved to Colorado from Illinois, and I got the feeling he was running away from something too, and his alcoholism seemed to come from as dark a place as I was coming from. Buying a bar as a recovering alcoholic seemed illogical, but, at the time, I was in no position to judge someone's logic.

After months of insanity, and without purpose, it was hard to adjust to a normal routine. Fortunately nothing about Gunnison was really normal, and my surroundings did not force me to be normal. This was a small town of less than ten thousand, more than a hundred miles from any interstate, with a liberal arts college, and a bunch of people who wanted to get away from mainstream America to live a different sorta life.

My return to climbing came in the form of my favorite medium—the indoor gym. There was a climbing gym right on campus, and I could sneak quick sessions in between classes. I had a tremendous amount of anxiety; I felt I was hiding something about my past, and how I got there, like I was a stranger in my own flesh, in a new, strange place. Climbing calmed my anxiety and transformed it into energy. The world forgives and forgets, especially when you are a young man, and, even if it took me a year to realize it, I'd been given a second chance.

The first sign of healing was that I no longer considered ending my life. I wanted to live even though I was so insecure I thought I'd never attract another woman. The second sign that I was improving my health, both mentally and physically, was that I wanted to stop using Dexedrine. Looking back, I'm sure that contributed greatly to my poor mental health, and it makes me sad that drugs like that were the solution to my problems. There was no one to blame though; my teachers and parents were just trying to get me through school, and that worked.

Though I picked out my courses quickly and erratically, I managed to sign up for a single credit mountain biking class. The entire class was held out at Hartmans, and I nearly died each class, forced to climb up a steep hill, dubbed Kill Hill, where, upon arrival at the top, I coughed for ten minutes straight, and each time it felt like demons were leaving my body. I chalked it up to cigarettes and told my classmates each time, "I gotta quit."

One day, my teacher announced he had some climbing gear for sale. I quickly expressed my interest, and, two sessions later, I had my first climbing rack in hand. That night I went over to a coworkers house, and we laid it out on the floor, staring at the gear, playing with it, discussing what type of adventures these camming devices would take us on. We marveled at the technology and simplicity, and we talked like young kids talk when they are readying for adventure, with no foundation of experience to plan said adventures.

Chapter 9

When I traveled home for Christmas that year, I could hardly mend the pain that I inflicted on my friends and family, but everyone seemed to want to move on. I was still incredibly closed off from my emotions, and I didn't discuss the inner turmoil that I'd just experienced. No one really wanted to bring it up anyway, so the talk was of the future. Caleb was planning on moving to Colorado, and I gave Tim a big speech on how he should move out as well.

Just before New Year's Eve, and the unnecessary hype that surrounded the transition into the 2000s that the Y2K computer bug was going to shut down the world, Tim and I headed down south to Carbondale where we planned to do some climbing in Jackson Falls. We met up with Geoff and his childhood friend Lane. Immediately upon arrival, we noticed something was off. Lane, who was a recovering heroin addict, was using methadone to fight his urges. He was sharing it with Geoff.

Geoff was completely opposite of the person I knew from a year before. His temper was high, and he was distraught. He demanded Tim share his weed and bullied him into smoking it. Usually content with mellow music like the Grateful Dead, he instead blasted Eminem, early Eminem and all the darkness that surrounded him, with lyrics about drugs, abuse, and self-loathing.

Out of darkness comes light. We headed into the forest that is Jackson Falls, unseasonably warm with only a hint of snow on the cliff and trees. Geoff was on the brink of insanity—we had one rope, fifty meters long, and he asked for it so that he could do a rope jump off the cliff where a waterfall cascaded in the summer, a mere trickle at the moment. We tried to talk him out of that, and he replied with explicatives that he knew what he was doing—he'd seen a Dan Osman video and wanted to try for himself. Geoff didn't know that Osman had died a year earlier in a rope-jumping accident, and we did our best to explain the situation. We were so frustrated with him, we eventually just handed him the rope to shut him up, and we went off on our own to do some bouldering.

We spent a couple hours in the magical play that is bouldering, and then met up with Geoff and Lane. Geoff didn't perform the rope jump, and we tried to explain that we were happy about that, but evil had come over him in the form of the pills—he'd eaten a dozen by that point—and his eyes were glazed over, and the Geoff that I knew, peaceful and thoughtful, was gone. We all packed in the car, with Geoff at the wheel, and decided we'd head back to Carbondale for New Year's Eve.

Geoff sped off in the car, and Tim and I, in the backseat, were terrified. Wide-eyed, we looked at each other and I pleaded to Geoff, "SLOW DOWN!"

Then Geoff turned the car into reverse and sped backward, and we really got freaked out. "STOP THE CAR!" I demanded.

And he did, and then he sped up again, veering off the road. He crashed into a tree. I was relieved the car had stopped. Then Geoff charged out of the car and started running up the dirt road. We watched in wide-eyed amazement as Geoff charged like an Olympic sprinter, disappearing off into the distance. He was gone.

We were so fed up with Geoff that we just let him go. I figured he'd be back in a little while, calmed down, and possibly down from the high. But, as the sun set and the final night of the nineties came upon us, he didn't come back.

So we built a fire and huddled around it with a bottle of rum. Though we were worried about our friend, the vibe was of intoxication, and there was a feeling of ending. The nineties were ending. And a feeling of beginning, and, more than anything in the world, I wanted new beginnings. And who offers a chance to start anew more than Mother Nature? The earth is just a series of endings and beginnings, green grass emerging from the ashes of sadness and failures.

The next morning we woke up weary, without supplies to cook a proper breakfast, so we hiked over to where Geoff's car was, started it up, and drove into Carbondale. The radio didn't seem to have any alarming news that the world was going to end, Y2K quickly faded from society's collective memory, and a new millennium was upon us.

We called Geoff from a pay phone, and he had hitchhiked all the way back home. When we knocked on his door, he acted like everything was normal. I was upset with him and didn't exchange too many words. We took the train back to Bloomington, and, a couple days later, I was back in Colorado.

Chapter 10

Winter was upon Gunnison, and I quickly learned that it was billed "The Coldest City in the Lower 48." Neither part of that statement is technically true. Gunnison isn't really a city, and there are other places that can contend for coldest. The truth in that little white lie is that Gunnison does get cold, really cold, like -30 cold, the type of cold you feel in your bones, the type of cold that freezes your car so that it won't start.

It didn't bother me that first winter. I was too in awe of the beauty of my first winter in Colorado. I would walk to class, smoking cigarettes, inhaling the coldest, purest air in between puffs of tobacco, floating across white snow, under the bluest sky my eyes had ever seen—an azure that led me to believe I was under a different sky than I was in the Midwest, the only place I'd ever known.

People seemed to huddle together in camaraderie of cold. Strangers would always say hello, and my teachers were not distant totem poles of education; they were the people I would also run into at the grocery store. Townie bikes were everywhere, even in winter, plowing through the snow, their riders covered from head to toe in warm clothes.

I had the opportunity to get deeper into winter when I signed up for a beginner recreation course. One day, we were all supposed to go snowshoeing near a wilderness area with a backdrop of snow-covered peaks amid large pine trees that carried a scent of a purity and an invigoration I could hardly put words to at the time.

Somehow I lost the group and was off on my own, one foot in front of the other in the magical white snow. And one foot in front of the other again. And again. A meditation came over me, and I had a vision. I would take another step toward cleaning out the deep, dark, hollow void that lived inside of me—I'd quit smoking cigarettes. The vision actually carried through, and, while the withdrawal of nicotine was unlike anything I'd ever experienced, the freedom of independence from a substance felt even better.

That recreation course took me even deeper into the heart of winter. One weekend, our class had to trek into the woods, where we would spend the night in snow caves. We skied in, and, quickly, as night approached, I found myself under the greatest array of stars my eyes had ever seen. Our homes for the evening would be snow caves, already constructed by another class the day before. Around the fire that night, the topics of conversation ranged from the skiing season to kayaking to mountain climbing in South America, but one guy had a story like no other.

Matty was a short, muscular body-building type of guy—after talking to him for only a few minutes, you would realize he was a guy you wanted on your side. He had a look of crazy but also a heart of gold. When the storytelling started around the fire, early twentysomethings were squeezing the juice out of the mere few years of real-life experience they had, and a few folks that had already known Matty's story begged him to tell it.

The summer before, Matty had been climbing in West Virginia and was a couple hundred feet above the ground, about to belay his partner up, when his anchor failed. Matty plummeted to the earth, landing on his head. He wasn't wearing a helmet, which he said somehow was advantageous; I think somewhere in his spirit he was part superhero. He didn't recall a thing from the accident, and he ended up with a huge metal plate in his head. All in all, he was a walking-talking miracle, and the last part of the story was how he was involved with the mountain rescue team at our college, ready to give back and save lives, just as his life was saved by a mountain rescue team earlier that summer.

We all looked at Matty as if he was a hero, and no one could come close to his story. That night, after the fire burned away, we watched the stars as long as one can watch stars, and we climbed into the snow cave. I slept restlessly because the cave made me claustrophobic, but it was also mind opening—in the heart of winter, in one of the coldest places in the United States, you could wander off into the woods and sleep comfortably in a structure made from snow.

Characters like Matty were commonplace in Gunnison, and I

was more than eager to hear their stories. One guy had ridden his bike from coast to coast, and another had climbed Mt. Everest. I'd never known people like this; after all, I was just a kid from Illinois. The athleticism oozing from every corner both intimidated and inspired me.

After winter passed, I invited Tim out for a visit. I was still terribly lonely and wanted a friend from home to move out to Gunnison. Tim seemed to be a perfect fit; he was less than happy with college life back in Illinois and wanted a change. I did my best to sell Gunnison as his future home. Caleb had already moved out to Colorado, north of Denver to a town called Fort Collins, and, when spring break rolled around, Tim scheduled a visit.

The arrival of spring stunned my heart. The life that sprang following the calm white stillness of the forever winter was filled with a re-energizing force I could try to poeticize—but I would certainly fall short. The azure of the sky seemed so pure, as if the world was a new place. Women were more alluring and attractive. There was an excitement that originated in nature, that rebirth and new beginnings were possible. And then there was granite, an infinite supply of rock in and around Gunnison—a place to practice your art of climbing.

I'd picked Tim up in the Front Range, near Denver, and we drove toward Gunnison. He was as dumbfounded by everything as I was. "Is that a ski resort?" he asked.

"No, that's just a hill," I replied.

Ten minutes later, "Is that a ski resort?"

"No, it's just another hill," I replied.

The Midwest lowers your expectations for geography and adventure so much that everything becomes something. Every little hill, every mountain pass, and every rock was worth taking in. We snapped photos like tourists. Tim had arrived, and I had a friend from home in a place I wanted to make my new home.

We sampled the local granite, and it tasted like freedom. The scene is always quiet in Gunnison, and, in the early 2000s, it was especially serene; all the college students were traveling the circuit that the climbing tribe visits, places like Hueco Tanks, Indian Creek, Joshua Tree, and Red Rocks, which were not quite yet in my lexicon.

I did my pitch for Tim to move to Gunnison, and, quiet as he was, I didn't get much out of him. He liked it though, and I could witness that in his eyes. When you brought Tim close to climbing, he had a different look, a thousand-mile stare, which brought you into the moment as well. We had finally arrived in the moment, which some people never find because they never discover something that makes their soul sing so much.

Just as Tim was about to head back to Illinois, we strolled through campus to show him the climbing gym. I noticed a flyer for an upcoming climbing competition. I had slowly been more attracted to outdoor climbing than gym climbing, but something deep inside me wondered if I could do well at a climbing competition, as if it could provide some sort of redemption for never succeeding in basketball. I would soon learn that climbing pays off in a different sort of way for most of us—a pay in poetry, a form of payment that takes a while to understand.

I entered the climbing competition and felt incredibly nervous about it. All around me were the characters I'd identified as climbers on campus, the shrugged shoulders that bore t-shirts with the names of climbing companies. Those characters whose hands were marked with white chalk, and whose vocabularies spoke wide-eyed of epics and beautiful summits. I was as scared of them as I was of exposure, the void.

I was hardly ready to compete and nervously climbed the first few boulder problems I attempted. My nerves were already shot three climbs in. I should have looked around and realized nobody cared. I already wasn't the worst climber; I had the perfect build, five-foot-nine, 150 pounds, and I was far from the best. And, at most climbing competitions at this sort of level, no one gives a shit anyway. It's all about getting together and having fun.

When I finally completed a problem, I dropped down to the pads, and a guy came up to me. He was obviously a climber, chalk covered his nose, and his arms could have been stolen from a quarterback. He greeted me with a "nice work, bro." My arms were shaking and as skinny as a waterboy's, and I wondered why this guy was being supportive? The "nice work, bro" felt so genuine, so inviting, it immediately made me feel more relaxed. As I reached out to shake his hand, it was like I was formally invited into this climbing world. No one in Illinois had this openness—this feeling that you, even though you were no one, could have someone bring you into this tribe. The guy was Ben Johnson.

After the competition, I felt the community of climbing for the first time, and I felt accepted, if for no other reason than that I found a community that is accepting in its nature. I only had a couple friends who climbed, and, when they weren't available, I'd take my crash pad and go bouldering by myself. Soon climbing was not merely sport; it sent my brain to a place of meditation, a sort of peace that I'd lost since I was a child.

As always, spring flowed into summer, and summer was even more spectacular. All I had to attend to was my schedule of washing dishes at work. A couple of climbers were hired there, and my social circle began to expand. One day, I called Caleb and told him how excited I was about climbing. Sensing my enthusiasm, Caleb suggested we go to the Wind Rivers in Wyoming and sample some granite in the wilderness. I countered that we should do something mellower, and a compromise was struck in the form of Devils Tower.

Devils Tower is one of those destinations, one of those rocks in the world that makes you think something divine happened there to create it. In the middle of the plains of Wyoming, it rises eight hundred feet in the air, a perfect cylinder of granite with cracks of all kinds going up it.

This was my first real climbing objective. I'd become infatuated with climbing over the previous year and a half, but this was my first time really putting anything to the test, to see if I could climb up into the sky, to see what was up there, and to see what might be within myself.

My memories of Devils Tower are hidden beneath more than a decade of other memories, hundreds of climbing days, a dozen lovers, a college degree, a million cups of coffee, yet somehow these memories, especially the day we climbed to the top, become crystal clear, like a mountain stream.

We spent our first couple days getting used to the stone, climbing up some single-pitch routes, just a hundred feet up the tower and then coming back down. Mountaineers might call it acclimatization; a rock climber doesn't really have a name for it, but feeling out the vibe of an area and getting comfortable on the rock is always a wise decision. Climbers usually perform best at areas they know well, familiarity leading to success.

So we spent a couple days getting comfortable. Caleb had already spent some time at Devils Tower when he was younger, so he was probably waiting for me to catch up to his level. After getting used to the cracks of the tower, we decided that we'd climb to the top.

Devils Tower seems like such a strange name for a place that has such an empowering energy to it. It is a sacred place to the native tribes, and every year it is closed to climbing for the month of June. That morning, we started up, and I was beginning to feel the energy more than ever. As we approached it, we were no longer just looking up at it—we were experiencing it. At the base of our selected route, Soler, we wrapped our hands in athletic tape and started up.

It was a hand crack, the kind of climb that swallows your entire hand and then you jam your feet in as well, and, when mastered, it feels as secure as vertical rock climbing can ever feel, like vertical hiking. At this point, I'd only climbed a few hand cracks, and my muscles weren't conditioned for it. Standing at the base of Devils Tower, with steep granite above my head, I was about to step out of my comfort zone and enter a world of something new.

To Caleb, this wasn't really a big deal; in fact, I think he'd done this route previously. For me now, I don't think it would be a big deal either, but that's not what climbing is about; it's about those moments you have on the rock—living in the moment, dealing with what fear comes up, and managing the situation, to success, or admitting that today is not the day, and backing off.

But that day was the day; there wasn't a cloud in the Wyoming sky, and the sun beat down on the tower as it has for years. I tied into the rope with a figure-8 knot, the knot of endlessness, and Caleb put me on belay. This was the steepest crack I'd ever led, and the hand jams were secure, but, the higher I got, the more desperate it felt. I dug deep within and kept jamming; I was giving it an effort that I'd never given a climb before. I was sweating and breathing heavily, and Caleb was sending up encouraging words as I hand jammed and slammed my rubber climbing shoes into the crack, inching up higher. The climb demanded more and more effort the higher I got, and I was at my limit, maybe past my limit. I breathed harder and harder, striving to hold on, as my arms became more and more pumped, exhausted. Suddenly, I was more in the moment than I'd ever been in my adult life, with my existence defined by my limbs being shoved into this granite crack. And then I could see the anchors: two bolts, above a small ledge, marking where I would belay. I mustered what strength and energy I had within, climbed to those anchors, and clipped in, attaching my rope to some carabiners.

A wave of emotion overtook me as I looked down the climb and out onto the plains—I cried tears of joy. I'd pushed my body and mind to the limit. I pulled up the remaining rope and put Caleb on belay. I was on cloud nine. When Caleb joined me I was about to express my joy, but, before I could, he started cursing about his shoes being uncomfortable.

Caleb led the next pitch, solidly jamming upward, and that was the end of the difficult climbing. It was nothing but scrambling up loose blocks on barely vertical terrain to the top. On top was a summit register, which we signed. I don't recall what I wrote, but there was a quote in it—"Climbing isn't worth dying for, but it is worth risking dying for."—from the great Wyoming climber Todd Skinner. Years later, Skinner would tragically die in Yosemite in a rappelling accident.

Caleb and I shared the moment of being on the football field sized grassy summit together. He'd brought me there, in more ways than one. He was the first person to take me climbing, and why he did, I'll never know, maybe just because I asked to, maybe because he needed someone to belay him. But either way, he shared climbing with me, just as climbers have always done with friends.

On the summit, I couldn't help but think of a story I'd heard about one of the first people to ever reach the top of Devils Tower, George Hopkins. It was the fall of 1941, and he was a parachutist who had jumped out of a plane onto the tower to win a fifty dollar bet. He'd hoped to make the descent with a rope that was dropped out of the plane, but something went wrong, and he was stranded atop the tower. The National Park Service began organizing a rescue, and weighed their options. Eventually, they accepted the offer of Jack Durrance, who had made the second ascent of Devils Tower in 1938, to lead the effort. Meanwhile, Hopkins had food, water, blankets, and a bottle of whiskey dropped to him, with assurance that help was on the way. He spent five nights alone on the summit. Imagine what he must have been thinking. These days, people climb up and down the tower all the time, but, at that point in history, only a handful of people had ever been up there. On day six, he was rescued by the team that Durrance led, with seven other climbers, and they led him safely down from the summit making several rappels.

Caleb and I shook hands, looked around some more at the unique panoramic view of the Wyoming plains, and rappelled down the tower.

After the climbing bug bit me on Devils Tower, I had it once and for all, and I also tried to see what else could give me a similar feeling. There's always a feeling of needing a new drug, and the next one I tried was kayaking, and then skiing, then ice climbing, but nothing did it for me like rock climbing.

I also, finally, had something to write about, and it poured out of me in the form of poetry. These were the best of times, the purest of times, and the poetry wrote itself. That memory of Devils Tower stood out above all other memories, and, back at college, in our library, I wrote out a poem. Nature complemented with education is a powerful force. When I was writing, as the great rapper Rakim once penned, "I was trapped, in between the lines," and I escaped when I finished the poem.

Writing is never finished and neither is climbing. The summit as a final page is an illusion. We are always writing that next poem and planning that next climb in our minds. This was a time of great romance and mystery, a time before every climb was recorded on the ether of the Internet and before there was much information available, other than books for climbing. My path was not set in stone, but, rather, the stone set my path.

Tim moved out that fall, and I felt the confidence of his presence, combined with my second year ever at a college. I decided I would study what inspired me—Recreation and Environmental Studies—and my path would unfold as it should from there.

Climbing with Tim changed everything. At first we were equals; our climbing ability remained the same once we both knew the basics. Then, all of a sudden, his abilities shot out like a rocket, and I was left holding on with one arm as the rocket blazed through space.

I followed Tim to granite all over the state, from our backyard climbs to Turkey Rocks in the South Platte region. I was amazed as he honed his abilities. He could dance on tiny holds, while he held on to finger locks, calm, cool, and collected. Sometimes I would have to remind him to place gear; he was just so confident he forgot. That was my role in those days: keep Tim alive, and keep myself alive.

Our circle of friends had grown by now—we were both working at restaurants, and I'd joined the college's rescue team. We had a crew. We did the usual things twenty-one-year-olds do, but, always and forever, the mission was climbing.

Tim had two jobs, so often I'd have to solicit other partners for climbing objectives. Jerid was a wide-eyed Colorado kid, who oozed passion and put climbing above everything else. He lived in the dorms, and a sticker tagged on a window as you approached his room read, "Climb Now, Work Later."

One day, he suggested we check out some climbs in the backyard of his boyhood home of Grand Junction. Even if the trip was an epic failure, we could visit his best friend Josh and eat food from his parents' cupboards.

Colorado National Monument, where we went climbing, was like something out of an old classic cowboy movie, full of red sand and stone. Jerid told me stories about how he and Josh would go climbing before they owned any proper equipment; they would just go out and climb and somehow emerge unscathed. Listening to those tales, I felt grateful I'd been given some proper instruction before I took the sharp end.

We found our way to the Devils Kitchen, a series of freestanding red rock formations rising seventy feet in the air, with some crack climbs here and there. We each had a couple of Camalots, spring-loaded devices that one can place into cracks and clip a rope to, which, when used correctly, will stop a fall. My grandmother had just given me two for Christmas a couple months before, and I was eager to use them. The three of us stared up at this crack, which started with hand jams and then moved left into a roof that had another crack running through it.

Somehow I ended up being the one who would lead it, so I racked up with all the gear we had. I climbed up the first thirty feet, jamming my hands and feet in the crack, and then moving left into the overhanging roof. As I hung from the roof, I had a desperate feeling that I needed to get some gear in. My last cam was fifteen feet down and five feet over to the right. The more I thought about my situation, the more I was losing control—that is what you need in the vertical, control, mastery, a feeling that you have a grip on the situation. I was hanging there, almost horizontal, and moved my hand out of the jam, and then I slipped.

Chapter 11

Death winked.

The end.

No control.

It happened so quickly. I was flipped upside down, and, in one brief instant, I hurled face first toward the ground. And then I looked to my belayer, Jerid. I was hanging five feet above the ground and looked into Jerid's eyes. I quickly flipped my self back around, and Jerid lowered me down to him. I looked at Josh and instantly hugged him. I cried from fear, but I was uninjured.

I flipped upside down because the rope was behind my legs when I moved into the roof. I'd made a very beginner mistake. I should have placed protection in the horizontal crack before moving into it. I was doing what many beginner climbers do, learning by mistake. But the mistakes in climbing are always attached to living or dying. I only lived out of chance, luck. Perhaps there were spirits looking after me, or perhaps I placed that cam at just the right location. A few more feet lower and I would have landed head first on the ground. Instead it was a thirty-five footer into the air. I never did tell Grandma that her Christmas gift saved my life.

My close calls weren't limited to climbing. One day, while driving to the nearby Black Canyon in Tim's purple truck, the roads were a little snowy. Something caught his eye, maybe a rock formation, or a bird. Quickly, we were veering toward a ditch. He over corrected, jerking the steering wheel to the left. Soon we were doing a 360 in the middle of the highway; he corrected again, and we spun another 180 degrees, and we stopped, in the other lane, facing the opposite direction. Luckily, we were on a sleepy highway of Colorado, and no other cars were coming. In my first couple of years out West, climbing, I had a streak of danger, but I came out of it unscathed.

Josh wasn't so lucky. He had problems with the law, and was on house arrest at the time, but he would, somehow, still get out to climb. He appreciated those moments so much, and I remember spirited conversations with him about all the places to climb on this great Earth. One day, after working his job waiting tables, he was on a ride with a friend on the back of his motorcycle. It was night, and who knows what happened; maybe they were going too fast or swerving to miss a deer, but they were thrown off the road. They both were killed. Jerid was devastated. His best friend was dead at twenty-one years old. And, just after attending Josh's funeral, Tim and I set out to Yosemite for the very first time.

Chapter 12

We soaked our pain in beer. I cried every time I was alone for a
week straight for Josh. Tim barely knew him, but he still went to the
funeral; that's just the kind of guy that Tim is. My state of mind was
clouded, lost, confused—when a young person dies, there's never an
answer to why?

I thought about bailing on the trip Tim and I had planned to
Yosemite. He wanted to go. We did. I think the best tribute a young
man could give to a fallen friend would be to stay on the path that
makes you happy. I was still figuring out if climbing was what made
me happy. Sometimes it did. Other times it freaked me out, made me
lose control, but, at this point, I was committed to another trip in the
purple truck, to a place Josh called The Promised Land in the last e-
mail he ever sent me. The last words he ever told me after we'd
climbed a tower in Colorado National Monument, "We're survivors.
We will survive."

The Western United States is a developed land, yet it is also very
wild. Especially when you hail from the Midwest as we did, where
there is very little wild land. Mountains and rocks had only been in
my life for a couple years—a new medium to which I was painting,
attempting to become an artist at living, which is what a dirtbag is at
his or her best.

There we were, farther west than we'd ever been, driving into
the Yosemite Valley for the first time. The drive is about sixteen
hours from Gunnison, twenty if Tioga Pass isn't open, or you make a
wrong turn. We must have slept on the highway that night, or maybe
Tim just kept driving; he could always put in some incredible hours
behind the wheel. Either way, we rolled in just as the sun was coming
up, a new day, a new chapter starting, and then there was the
presence of El Capitan, impossible to ignore, and I knew I was a long
way from home.

El Capitan soars so high that it takes the brain some moments to
figure out what it's seeing. But there was no mistaking that it was El
Cap. Three thousand feet of rock—light golden granite, just sitting

there, beaming in the early morning light. Though I know I felt fear just being in its presence, there was something special, something spiritual, to be there in that moment.

I was in a daze and probably had that dumb expression that tourists do when they first see El Cap. They stop their cars, sometimes in the middle of the road, and just start staring at it, dumbfounded. Immediately they become hazards to the busy traffic, but they don't care. They just have to stare at El Cap. They don't know why.

On the other hand, Tim had that look in his eyes that a climber gets when he sees a place he must get to. An intense focus rose to the surface of his being, and I could sense it. His eyes were wide open and ready for whatever Yosemite could throw our way. He immediately wanted to experience the walls. There would be no delay. He wanted to select a route and start climbing.

I simply wanted to survive. In the last year, since he'd moved to Colorado, he'd progressed so quickly that there had to be some metaphysical reasons, something beyond him that explained why he was so comfortable on the rock. He'd mastered all the basics so quickly that he could float any 5.10 out there. My duty in these situations was so try to advise Tim to keep safe, to suggest putting more gear in when he was running it out. He was always so zoned in on the rock that sometimes he'd feel so secure on the holds and in the jams that he would simply forget to place gear. When I climbed, I placed as much gear as possible, sometimes too much, and I'm sure he would get frustrated with my slow progress when he could get up the climb much faster. But we were a team, united by circumstance and friendship, and he was stuck with me.

At the start of the trip, Tim would suggest a big climb, and I would come up with excuses why I wasn't ready and suggest something less difficult. This happened over and over again, and, at one point, Tim got frustrated and blurted out that he would maybe find another partner. But that was just his eagerness to leap into the vertical world of Yosemite and experience its vibration and beauty. Eventually we had a list of classics we would do, and each day we'd line up at the base of one of them and embark upward.

After success on a couple classics like Nutcracker and the Central Pillar of Frenzy, I crossed that threshold of fear and entered into obsession. Yosemite was paradise. Everywhere, seemingly perfect walls soared into the heavens. I pondered staying, forever. The grassy meadows were beautiful too, as was the lazy, wide Merced River. Tim and I had found some satisfaction climbing together, and, though I'm sure he wanted to try harder climbs, he seemed content. Soon our week there was coming to an end, so we picked a big rock to climb—Half Dome.

I built up nervousness about Half Dome, like I'd always do with a long route. My mind always played tricks on me in the beginning. Maybe it's a natural thing to do; while deep in our ancestry, we may have been climbing, tree-dwelling species, climbing big vertical rocks is entirely new for human beings.

While El Cap sits right there in the heart of Yosemite Valley, close enough that just about anyone could walk up and touch it, Half Dome sits seven miles away from the Valley, close enough to see, but it takes an effort to get to. It has a sheer two-thousand-foot vertical face that lies in the shade for most of the day. A golden face with hints of orange and shades of gray. It stands proudly, suggesting an adventure, close to the Valley, yet far away. We were intrigued.

Snake Dike was our objective: a slab of rock running up the southwest face of Half Dome, skirting the vertical face that stands out from the Valley, but still leading one to the summit, fourteen miles of hiking round trip, with a thousand-plus feet of slab climbing.

The way to do this climb is to bust it out in one big day. Get up early, make a light rack, and get 'er done. We didn't know this, so we decided to hike up the night before, and camp out close to the base of the route, then climb the route the following day. I was all sorts of nervous because Snake Dike supposedly had long runouts without gear. We hiked up the winding trail and found a place to camp near the base of the route. Soon we heard the clinking of climbing gear and the chatter of other people. It was a family of five, a Dad and four kids, ranging from six to thirteen. They'd just climbed the route, and had left some gear at the base that they needed to retrieve. In that moment, I realized the ridiculousness of my fears—if a six-year-old could get up the climb, I probably could too.

That night was the most memorable of my life. We knew we couldn't bring a full camping setup because it would be too heavy, so we went light. As night approached, I crawled into my sleeping bag and looked over to Tim, expecting him to do the same. He decided not to bring a sleeping back and just stoically looked back at me. There we were, two best friends sleeping on a rock together. We shared a can of beans, the only food we brought for dinner. Then it was silent.

We fantasized about food, and, up until that moment, I don't think I'd ever appreciated food like that. It was always just there. And now it wasn't. We made a deal that, when we got back to Gunnison, we would make a trade from the two places we worked at. We were both dishwashers at neighboring restaurants. Under the stars, we talked about food some more and then silently drifted off, me into a somewhat restless but sheltered sleep, and Tim into his own world of sleeping on a rock, with little protection from the elements—a hat, a pair of pants, and a fleece. He didn't complain one bit. Cold ground was our bed that night and rocks our pillows, another world within our world opened up.

We started with the sun and found our way to the beginning of Snake Dike, named after a dike formation that the climb leads to. With the presence of the family that had climbed the route the day before, my fear had calmed down but then came back as we were roping up at the base. Climbing offers excellent opportunities to deal with fear: you must face it or back off.

The start was pure slab climbing, which involves delicate dancing on the rock, mostly staying on the tips of your feet as you move across the stone. Tim led the first traversing pitch, and then it was my turn. I started off, my fear right there with me following each step, reminding me what I was doing. I would always get more nervous when there was more air beneath me, the farther I was above a bolt or a piece of protection. This is where fear must be managed; you must remain in the moment and delicately balance on the rock. I had a moment where I was frozen, scared to make any movement, but worked through it. I didn't want to become a statue on the rock, and

I wanted to end this trip on a good note. Once I reached that second belay, we were at the start of the really easy climbing up the dike. The holds running up the dike were the size of mailboxes—you would have to *try* to fall off of them. We ran up those dikes, and it was impossible to fall. It was a joyous feeling, and they went on for hundreds of feet. At the top of Half Dome, I thought maybe I was born to climb after all.

There's a unique interaction when one is out of the vertical and into a place that tourists inhabit. Half Dome is climbed up the back side by thousands every year, and we immediately left the solitude of climbing and entered a scene with lots of people who'd just hiked to the top. When you have a rope and climbing gear, you're suddenly like an animal in a zoo or something, but an animal that can be asked questions. They are all the same.

"How did y'all get the rope up there?"

"Now are the bolts placed in the rock or do you have to place them as you go?"

"What do you do if you have to go to the bathroom?"

I always do my best to politely answer these questions, but then there comes a time when you get sick of it, and you just want to get out of there.

Getting off of Half Dome is a trip because the descent goes down The Cables—a series of pipes driven into the rock long ago, which is the route that the hikers go up and then down. It's third class, mostly low angle, but steep enough that the average person needs some assistance to get up, and most people appreciate them on the way down. We were draped in climbing gear, and the tourists kept asking us questions, "Did you climb the big face?"

I wanted to answer yes, but, no, we just climbed the slab around the corner of it. And then there were the freakouts. Someone would get out of their comfort zone and lose it. A woman yelled at her husband, "You didn't tell me about this, Bob. I want to go down!"

Once one person gets scared, the fear builds, and more people get scared. We just wanted off this damn thing. Once off the cables, it's seven miles down, past a marching parade of hikers at their limits, fatigued, dehydrated souls, determined to get to the top of Half Dome. This scene is played out season after season in the crowded wild land that is Yosemite.

When it was time to leave Yosemite, I couldn't have been happier. I was pushed to my limit with hiking and climbing, and I hadn't gotten much sleep over the course of that week. When we got back to the Valley floor and packed up the purple truck for the journey back to Colorado, a rush of relief washed over me. Fears were faced, and obstacles were overcome. We drove out of there on a high, past El Capitan, and out into the highways of the West, back home.

Chapter 13

Only when it is dark enough can you see the stars.

—*Martin Luther King Jr., "I've Been to the Mountaintop"*

Once we were home, in Gunnison, Tim and I both decided to move into tents. We'd heard of other climbers doing this, and it made sense to save money. I also took a semester off from college—I was about to earn in-state tuition and figured it would financially make sense to hold that diploma off a mere few months.

Originally, Tim and I had planned to camp together, but life was already stretching us apart, as it often does for friends. Most of his work was up north in Crested Butte, and my job was down in Gunnison. We tried to find campsites in between, looking for protected nooks in forested canyons, but, ultimately, we camped alone.

My piece of real estate was at Hartmans. My possessions consisted of those that could fit in my car. I had distilled life down to something I'd only dreamed of, like Huck Finn was whispering advice on how to live life.

From the tent was my view of home, rusty-and-golden granite boulders and domes, rising ten to fifty feet from a floor of rolling hills among teal-colored sagebrush. A sky so blue, it was often hard to believe that this is the sky we are all living under, and moderate amounts of wildlife were present: bunnies hopping; squirrels coming and going in their erratic ways; blue birds flying from sagebrush to sagebrush, never losing sight of one another; the occasional deer; coyotes that are heard more than seen; and mountain lions that are rarely heard and even more rarely seen. A bear might also pass through this land occasionally, but it would have been a bear that lost its way, as this was a desert sagebrush land, far from the rivers and forests that a bear needs.

My tent was right next to a granite boulder that, from one angle, looked like a brain, so that's what I called it. I would tell people, "I live right next to The Brain." It was one of the many boulders in my backyard that I would climb, with razor edges destined to cut climber's fingers for eternity, which would also cut into the rubber on a climber's shoes. This was home. Every night, I would sit by a comforting, modest fire, under the stars unseen by many in this modern world, and, every morning, I would wake up by the sun, leading me to another day of this life.

When I woke up, I immediately craved human interaction. I enjoyed the quiet nights inside my head, but it never took long for me to miss people. So I'd always end up in a coffeeshop or breakfast joint where I would warm up and talk with whomever I'd see that I knew. When I didn't do that, I would write. I would write for the sake of writing, often scribbling poetry on napkins or scrambling for a sheet of paper wherever I could.

I was making peace with my creator. Climbing, school, and friends had helped to heal the wounds from my meltdown that had led me out West, but there was still a lingering pain. I read somewhere once that "you never really get over anything." Of course its poetic, and only in poetry do you really find truth; the truth was that I was still suffering.

At night, I talked to God. My notion of a Christian God had long ago faded. Sure, that added up the list of my American mind that I was a failure. According to the checklist for American success, my waning belief in the Christian God was one of the things that pointed to my failure. Success in America: study hard, follow the way of the Bible, get married, have kids, be good so you get into heaven. Die. Get to heaven. A successful life.

I'd argued my point of view before, and, though I had the instinct of conviction, I wasn't entirely sure what I believed; I just knew I was rejecting something. For me, that was the problem of being a hippie—it was all about rejection. I was pushing out all the philosophies, but I was bringing nothing back in.

In the still of the night, with the ocean of sky and bright shining stars above, something started coming in. We give something a name, but, in reality, a name is just what we come up with. There are many languages, many beliefs, but we all live under this one sky.

The flickering of the fire was my television; the stars were my muse. I wrote poetry, or, rather, the poetry wrote itself. It really did. The morning sun delivered another day. I would journey into town. I would work, eat, build friendships, climb, run, and then do it all over again. I was the happiest I'd been in my adult life. I was in love with life, and part of me was able to come to the realization that I could find some purpose within my life.

Soon I'd settled on one place as my morning hangout. My car had broken down, and I was entirely reliant on my own two feet. And my thumb. I saw others who needed rides, sticking their thumbs out, hitchhiking, and it seemed to work. So I did the same, and people would stop, and, as the season progressed and the temperatures dropped, the people who picked me up would question my motivations. They were surprised I was living out of a tent, with a broken down car, exposed to the elements. I liked that surprise; it was like the shock of someone having dreadlocks, something so different from normal Americans that it made people take notice. I had a purpose, and the purpose was to commune with nature, with a rock as my pillow and the world as my home.

At this morning hangout—the Firebrand: a coffeeshop, morning breakfast joint, and deli—the needs of the Gunnison people were served through multitasking, as a small town restaurant will do. My scraggly, unshaven, unshowered appearance was hard to ignore, yet I fit in perfectly.

One day, the owner finally recognized me as a regular. It was the simplest of gestures—she gave me a reusable container for my tea, trusting me with returning it and not throwing it away. The gesture made me feel at home, and I realized that I had arrived home, again. Home was not some fixed point—home was in the heart. That morning, I was home. I scribbled out some more poetry on a napkin and fell into a deep meditation of loving simplicity, hospitality, and nature.

At home, at my campsite, I was rebuilding my life, in my heart and in my mind. Sure, I was as poor as dirt, and I didn't technically have a home, but that was perfect. I had no attachment. I was practicing my own religion, my own philosophies, and they were not force-fed to me—I chose them. Later, I would learn a word for my lifestyle, *dirtbagging*, but even just writing out that word seems to compromise the clarity I felt in those days.

Chapter 14

There's been rumors of war and wars that have been

The meaning of life has been lost in the wind

And some people thinkin' that the end is close by

'Stead of learnin' to live they are learnin' to die

Let me die in my footsteps

Before I go down under the ground

—Bob Dylan, "Let Me Die In My Footsteps"

Then, when all seemed like peace had been restored to my existence, 9/11 happened. I was out on a morning jog, something I'd added to my climbing training, and I was listening to the radio on my Walkman. The song on the radio was interrupted: the United States had been attacked, and the first World Trade Center had fallen. I went into the grocery store and ran into a friend. "We're going to war," he said.

I gathered with all the other college kids in the student union. Everyone was shocked, and there was a major sense of confusion. Sadness was all about. I had lunch with a friend at The Firebrand; we talked about how we were going to war. I thought society was going to shut down, and, after lunch, I went to the grocery store and absurdly spent the remaining twenty dollars I had on ramen noodles. At work, we watched the TV coverage, and spoke to one another with the kind of care humans do after this sort of tragedy. That night, I drank beer with friends, and I fell asleep on someone's floor.

September 11th stunned America, and, in our remote mountain refuge of Gunnison, we felt it too. Of course, society did not shut down, and my feeling that it was going to shut down showed me how little I truly knew about the world and how it functioned. Our leader at the time, George W. Bush, didn't seem to understand the workings of the world either, showing this by his inarticulate language and flexing of the military muscle in regions that had nothing to do with 9/11, while he lied and staked his case for war and set a course that I was saddened and confused by. With all of that going on, I was still determined not to sink into depression and to follow this new path. I'd already set sail on a new journey, and nothing short of death would stop it.

This world of machinery and war, it's all too much, isn't it? If there is a God who created us and is watching over us, God surely did not give us this life to fight so much, right? If I were still in Illinois, I know I would have sunk deeper into a darkness, given the coming war, but I had seen the light already, and the light came from the sun, and, if you were in the right place (nature) at the right time (sunrise or sunset), well, there was a certain beauty to it that made you believe. Believe in what? Hope.

And where do you find hope? Bob Dylan asked us that a long time ago in his epic poem "Last Thoughts on Woody Guthrie." His answer, his hope, in the poetic way only Dylan can communicate, was in Woody Guthrie, as he lay dying in the Brooklyn State Hospital, and it was in the Grand Canyon at sundown. My hope was in the sunrise at Hartmans, as it awakened me every morning. It was in Yosemite, a place I truly regarded as a Promised Land that could save the lost soul. Hope was also in the red rock desert of the Colorado Plateau. Moab. Hope was in the desert.

We called it *the desert* when, in reality, Gunnison and my home at Hartmans was its own desert, a sagebrush-foothills sort of desert, but when you're talking time and place, the time being the early 2000s and the place being the Moab desert, THE is where the emphasis is, because, when compared to any other desert for climbing, in the United States there is only truly one that stands supreme.

I'd had my first trip to the desert in 1999 over Thanksgiving. Caleb had invited me there and had given me some basic directions. I spent my first night cold, sleeping in my car at a quiet, frozen campground along the river. In the morning, I drove more into the canyon, and found a small dirt pullout where I would meet Caleb and his friends. When I hiked up to the wall, I noticed a climber seventy feet up a perfect crack, untethered from a rope. Not wanting to break his concentration, I quietly hiked past him. My naïve mind figured that was something normal, free soloing desert cracks.

When I found Caleb and the crew, I did the thing that I always do—I tied into the rope and tried a climb. Crack climbing is a masochistic art, and I fumbled and fought to learn how to insert my fingers, my hands, and my feet into the crack. Figuring this out was the hardest thing in the world, and, when I looked around at the others who had practiced and mastered this art, I was 100 percent sure I would never reach that level of technique and athleticism.

I arrived at the wall with my very basic climbing set up. I wore sweatpants and had a harness, a belay device, climbing shoes, and a fifty-meter rope. The innocence and lack of knowledge about climbing was oozing from my pores, mostly the sweatpants, and the gawking coming from my face. I knew what to do though—offer someone a belay, and later I would have a toprope set up.

One of the guys in the crew, who was British, wanted a belay; climbing is perhaps the best way to make a genuine connection with someone from another country. So I belayed. The climb was Fingers In A Light Socket, a finger crack, which finished at some desperate face moves, sixty feet up, and it's one of the only climbs at the buttress you could actually use a fifty-meter rope on. He got to the crux, the difficult face moves, and hung on a cam. Eventually he figured out the moves, and, after a couple more hangs, he set up a toprope.

It was my turn to climb, but, just before I was about to tie in, the free solo guy emerged out of nowhere. He seemed high on adrenaline and wanted another fix.

He eyed our climb, and, after confirming we didn't mind that he tried it, he climbed up, untethered to anything in this life, with only the tips of his fingers in the crack and the tips of rubber from his climbing shoes inserted into the wall.

Indian Creek is a crazy place, I thought to myself as I watched the madman climb alongside my blue rope, which was barely wavering from side to side in the light breeze.

He was fine for the first forty feet, and then he started to look shaky. *Oh my fucking God, am I going to watch a guy fall to his death during my first hour at Indian Creek?* I wondered.

My new British friend looked at me, not wanting to say anything but gravely concerned. Then, like it's nothing, he gave up his free solo attempt, grabbed on to my rope, and then climbed down it, back to our perch on the ground. He mumbled something about how hard it was, and then disappeared into the day. Fifteen years later, as I write this, I've yet to see another person free solo in Indian Creek.

That next day there were some climbers, obviously Creek veterans, who were establishing a new route. I didn't even really notice what was going on until they reached the top of the crack, and there were no anchors. So, they hauled up a power drill and swiftly drilled two holes, and then hammered expansion bolts into the wall. Most of the climbs I'd done had the same anchors, but this was the first time I'd witnessed a new route go up. Whoever said there's nothing new under the sun was not a climber. For the rest of my life, I know there will always be new routes; you just have to know where to look. In the late 1990s there was more low-hanging fruit out in the Colorado Plateau than there is now, but the fruit is still ripe for the picking.

Flash forward a couple years, and we were just getting the taste for a desert fix.

I'd figured out the techniques, the basics, and spent plenty of time paying my dues, jamming every type and size of crack I could find. The adrenaline and endorphins that desert climbing creates is addicting, so much that we found ourselves returning as often as possible, striking while the iron was hot, and the nights were cool.

Tim was the ropegun, the energy I attached my climbing hopes and dreams to. He was a force to be reckoned with, and he was always the secret weapon we used as we climbed harder and harder.

Around this time, Tim became Two Tent Timmy. When I

moved into a tent in Gunnison, Tim moved into a tent in Crested Butte, the epic mountain town 30 miles north of Gunny, where he was working at the time. Some friends went to visit him at his new home, a piece of real estate on National Forest land that he staked out by setting his tent up. What he did, that everyone thought was so memorable, was he put a tent inside another tent. The larger outer tent was where he kept his cooking supplies and other gear, and the inside tent was where he slept. Once the words Two Tent Timmy were uttered, it was a nickname for life.

This was perfect because there was another Tim. We worked together, and he was on the mountain rescue team, and he was interested in climbing. We struck a deal: I would join the rescue team and learn from him and his life-saving compadres, and we would teach him some things about climbing.

So, one day, Two Tent, Tim (the new Tim) and I were at Supercrack Buttress in Indian Creek, talking about what we were going to do the next day. A climber was eavesdropping, listening in to the process. He said, wisely, "You guys should check out the North Six Shooter."

We inquired. Obviously we knew the formation—it was the most striking tower in all of Indian Creek: a slim crimson pistol that stood all alone, shot four hundred feet in the air and hovered there like a beacon.

We probably muttered some questions, asking about the crux and the gear, but what I remember most is his convincing statement: "It doesn't get any better than the North Six Shooter."

That night at camp, we looked through the guidebook, scribbled out a topo map of the pitches, and tried to hide our nervousness. Two Tent wasn't nervous though. He lived for this stuff. It was like, at any time, he was ready to face his fears and try his hardest on the rock. I was usually in the opposite realm, unready to face my fear and hopeful that something would come up, so we could give up and get stoned, go back to the comfort zone. Secretly though, deep inside, I wanted to face my fear with confidence like Two Tent did. I wanted to live freely.

We drove Tim's truck toward the mighty North Six Shooter. A few clouds hovered off in the distance, a storm brewing for sure. One of us mentioned cancelling the mission for cragging at the Supercrack Buttress again, but Two Tent's persistence and vision carried us through the drive to park the truck, and we began hiking up. We totally blew the approach, and it took us two hours instead of one, often hiking on ball bearings, the point on a talus cone where the surface is unsteady, unpredictable, and you feel like you're going to tumble down to certain injury if you slip.

Sweaty, already tired, confused, and disoriented, I looked up at the tower. There are only two main routes, and they are so obvious that a grandma with cataracts could point them out. Our intended line, the Lightning Bolt Cracks, shot up, and zigged and zagged back and forth, so divine, and perfectly shaped for the human fingers, hands, and feet, it was crazy to think they'd only first been climbed just after we were born. Since the gear, the camming devices necessary to protect cracks like these, was only invented in 1978, nearly every climb in the desert was done first in our lifetimes. (The ones that were done previous to this were mostly easy or dangerous endeavors, completed by pioneers that led the way to a golden age that is currently riding high.)

The other line, Liquid Sky, was a brutal overhanging squeeze chimney, even more obvious than the Lightning Bolt Cracks. I'd read about the climb in a magazine, and it had such a daunting reputation that a thousand people look at it, for every one that tries it. The major rumor was that you could become stuck in it, and, if you fell, you would fall so deeply into it, you could die, and they would never be able to retrieve your body. Rumors are rumors though. But I've yet to climb that thing, so I can't confirm or deny.

Two Tent racked up with our meager selection of gear, though growing by the day. That's something about climbing—your gear, especially if you're a dirtbag, is the most expensive of your possessions. When you embark on a climb, you pool up all your gear, and it becomes one communal thing. Two Tent went up with everything and navigated his way through the first crack system, eventually pulling through an overhanging off-width squeeze. Then he slowed down.

Two Tent was rarely slowed down, and Tim and I noted the rope coming to a halt. We looked at each other and whispered what we were thinking. I was belaying and kept my focus on being ready for Two Tent to fall, and Tim had his eyes on the weather; the clouds were building and building, and he mentioned that a thunderstorm was inevitable.

It was, and, just as Tim suggested it, thunder started.

Exposure is a big concept in climbing. Sometimes exposure means two thousand feet of air beneath your climbing shoes; at this particular moment, we were exposed to lightning. The instinct is to get the hell out of there, but I was tethered to Two Tent, holding the rope for his belay, and he was facing a thin, blank section, trying to wiggle in gear, but nothing fit. We yelled back and forth, and he decided to down climb to a chockstone, wedged into the wide crack he'd just passed. The chockstone had some webbing around it, and he clipped a biner to it and lowered down to our perch. Thunder clapped all around, and, finally, it was time to book it.

We scurried off the hill, slipping and sliding, but making it swiftly back to the truck, while thunder and lightning erupted all around us. Just when we got back to the truck, it really let loose. The heavens were purple, with a hundred flashes of lightning going off at a time, thunder erupting so often, you couldn't tell what lightning was connected with what thunder. As we drove away, we couldn't have been happier to be in the truck, and the majestic desert was soon in the rear view mirror as we headed back to Gunnison.

As winter approached in Gunnison, we had a burning desire to see a little more before all the rocks were covered in snow. So, we headed back to Yosemite, just before Thanksgiving Day.

This time there were four of us in that purple truck. We were joined by Jerid and Dane, who was the newest member of our crew. Dane was equally as innocent and optimistic as we were; he loved climbing and was intoxicated by it, just as we were.

It was a colossal mistake to have so many people in such a small truck, but it was indicative of the lengths we would go to experience the climbing life. This was just a two-seater, so at least two people would be uncomfortable at all times. For twenty hours, we rotated in this manner: three in the front, with someone sitting bitch, or two in the back and two in the front. It was uncomfortable, unsafe, but we arrived in Yosemite unscathed.

This time I was more than willing to jump on the walls right away upon our arrival. I'd been dreaming about the granite of Yosemite for months and couldn't wait to experience it again. Tim and I got on the Royal Arches, a fifteen-hundred-foot moderate route that climbs to the left of some giant arch formations on low angle terrain, with a great view of Half Dome to the east. At one point, we got passed by three soloists, climbing without ropes, smiling; one of them was even barefoot, with a thousand feet of air below him.

By the time we reached the top, we were relatively fatigued. We'd made that marathon drive, during which we drank little water and ate nothing but junk food, and then we hopped right on the wall. At this point, we had to make a series of rappels, heading down the descent slab and then into a chimney system to finish things off.

By the time we reached the chimney, it was dark. I was feeling nature's call, and really had to poop. I wanted off the damn wall, and I got in a hurry. I saw a fixed rope leading to the next rappel and decided to hop on that instead of rigging our own rope. I rappelled down the rope, looking for the next bolted anchor, and then, all of a sudden...

SNAP!

The end of the rope went through my rappelling device.

Chapter 15

Since I was in a chimney, I barely moved an inch.

I was shocked, but there was no time to contemplate what had just happened. My instincts told me to reach up and get back on that rope. I did and instinctively climbed back up the rope using a prusik. If I weren't in that chimney, I would have fallen three hundred some feet down the wall, with probable death, and, if I wouldn't have died, it would have been worse than death.

Another close call avoided, we rigged our own ropes up for the rappel and made it safely back to the ground. Once on the ground, we tried to pull the ropes, and they became stuck. It was pitch dark. We had two options: climb up the ropes using a prusik, or just leave the ropes until the morning and deal with it then. We chose the latter and then went to find our shoes and jackets at the base where we started. We couldn't find the base.

Frustrated and draped in nothing but ropes and climbing gear, still wearing our climbing shoes, we set out to find Jerid and Dane. We caught a bus to the Curry Village where we thought we were supposed to meet. No sign of them. They had the purple truck, which had all our sleeping gear in it. So we just sat by a fire in the Curry Village, warming up and trying to figure out what to do. We didn't have cellphones, so we just had to simply wait to see if they would come by. There was an Alcoholics Anonymous conference that weekend, and there was bustling traffic throughout the building. Many of them noticed our climbing gear and stopped to ask us questions as we pathetically sat there waiting for our friends.

Now this was a dirtbag moment. We started to think about what might happen if we didn't meet up with Dane and Jerid. We needed to figure out where we would sleep. We only had a couple dollars in our pockets, which we spent on tea to warm ourselves up. We'd have to find a place to sleep. We contemplated crawling under some tables in the coffeeshop area and hiding there when they closed down for the night. Things were getting desperate. A couple hours passed, and there was no sign of our friends. Finally we decided to catch the last bus to the Awahnee Hotel, which has the finest accommodations in Yosemite, and try to sleep on couches in the lobby. Still clothed in all our climbing gear, we found our way to the Awahnee.

We got off the bus and walked through the cold night into the Awahnee. I have no idea how we even made it past the door, looking like the dirtbags that we were, but we were soon out of the cold and into the classy hotel. It was decided that Tim would sleep on the first floor, and I would go to the second. I headed up the stairs and planted myself on a couch in the lobby. I fell into a restless sleep, wearing climbing shoes and using a rope for my pillow. Poetic, yet far from comfortable.

I woke up in the morning and quickly found my way out of the hotel. Two Tent was waiting for me near the entrance. He had been discovered in the early morning and was asked to leave. So he went to the base of the Royal Arches and retrieved our shoes. I changed shoes and thanked him. We laughed about our night but didn't talk about my near-death miss on the rappel. We didn't bring it up for years.

I tell the story often now, especially to younger climbers. Though I don't know if telling it really saves anyone from danger, but it reminds me how delicate life is, and how everything after that day is a bonus, because in all reality I should have paid the price for my mistake. And that price should have been death, finding out what is after this life.

Eventually we found Dane and Jerid; they were waiting at the Yosemite Village, and we were at Curry Village, a simple confusion that led to our adventurous bivouac at the five-star hotel.

We still had to retrieve our ropes, which were stuck on the last rappel. I climbed up the ropes with a prusik. Looking around that pleasantly warm and bluebird late November day, I thought again about my mistake, yet I had no plans to abandon climbing. The rational decision might have been to give it up. All these near-death experiences for what? A rush? What was I discovering by existing in the vertical? Questions unanswered then, perhaps unanswered forever—more question marks in the rabbit hole that is climbing philosophy.

The knot of the ropes was stuck in a crack. I removed the knot and then rappelled back down to the ground. We pulled the ropes and then had the inevitable conversation you have when any adventure is done: What will we climb next?

As we thought about that, I was wrought with guilt on the inside for my mistake. I'd now had two near-death experiences in that year alone. I thought of my parents and how they would have dealt with my death. I would be another young climber dead in Yosemite.

Internally, I could not move on from that, and I think about that day still all the time. Luck was on my side again. Physically, we moved on. Since no one was in Yosemite, we went over to El Capitan and did a couple pitches at the base. We climbed three pitches up on the Salathe

Wall, one of the trade routes on El Cap. There were frogs in the cracks, and they seemed inviting, like, hey, come see what's up here. Touching The Captain felt magical. We rappelled, safely, with thousands of feet of granite above us, promising future adventures, if we could only stay alive.

The next day we woke up, and it had snowed. That was how we got our weather forecasts then. We woke up and looked outside our tents. Winter had officially arrived, and it was time to go back home. On Thanksgiving Day, we camped on some public land just outside of Las Vegas. We had no money and ate beans and cheap sausages. We shared a forty of Olde English, a malt liquor. At one point, the pot slipped off our poor little stove, and the beans fell into the dirt. When we ate the beans for dinner, rocks crunched in our mouths. We might as well have been hobos, or gypsies, living on the road, with just enough money and supplies to sustain ourselves for another day.

Chapter 16

A snowy, magical road of twists and turns led us back to Gunnison. Jerid took the wheel, a Colorado boy who knew how to handle a two-wheel-drive truck in the snow. The two in the back, Two Tent and Dane, acted like sandbags, keeping us from skidding off the road to certain disaster.

Near-death experiences rarely resolve themselves. Almost everyone has one at some point in their lives. I never had that feeling of being closer to God, or some light at the end of the tunnel, but, a week after I rappelled off the end of my rope, we were gambling once again, driving this small, overloaded purple truck over a mountain pass—everything felt fucking magical.

So we arrived back to Gunnison. Two Tent and I were still homeless. Homeless in December in the coldest city in the country. The morning we arrived home, we went to a breakfast joint. I felt warm in the heart, like I was a nestled child in my mother and father's home. Gunnison was the home. Every dirtbag should have some place they call home.

Friends took us in, and we crashed out on floors. We were in love with this experience, not knowing where we might stay that night but having complete faith someone would take pity on us. Places where dirtbags inhabit have these intricate systems of karma and hospitality built within their fabrics. The greatest thing about it all—we discovered it on our own; no one told us, growing up, that they existed, and to have found it seemed like discovering the greatest treasure of all.

My car. I'd forgotten about it. Was it the weed, or the carelessness, or being so in love with being a dirtbag that nothing but the moment mattered? I left my car at Hartmans at my campsite when I left for Yosemite.

One day, the police arrived at the restaurant, asking for me. I'd just taken a hit of weed and blown the smoke into the vents of the kitchen, and the last thing anyone in the world wants to hear is that the police are looking for you after you just got stoned.

"Are you Luke Mehall?" they asked.

"Um, yeah."

"Why has your car been abandoned at Hartman Rocks?"

"Well it broke down, and I need to get it fixed."

"Okay, you need to do that. Now, another matter, why is there a bag of marijuana in your car?"

My heart sank into my gut. Was I really that careless to leave a bag of weed on the front seat of my car? Weed is legal now in Colorado, but back then it was far from legal. They wouldn't fine you heavily and put you on probation like they do in Utah, but you would still get a ticket and owe a couple hundred bucks. And that much money then was a small fortune to me.

The police confiscated my driver's license and gave me a number to call when the car had been removed. That night it snowed a foot. Hartmans closes its gates for the winter when the snow rolls in, and the land is reclaimed by snow and wildlife. I had to call a tow truck driver, as well as the Bureau of Land Management to open the gate, so that my car could be towed out.

Dirtbag climbers and government authorities are constantly at odds. We, the dirtbag climbers, claim the land with rocks as our own, a civil disobedience of sorts. The government wants to limit our camping stays to two weeks, while we feel these areas are our homes, and we should be able to stay as long as we want. The world is controlled by the rich, who consume and rape nature and build mansions, and all we want to do is pitch a tent, have adequate food and water, and climb rocks. The noblest culture I've been a part of to date in my life.

In Yosemite, there's a long history of climbers and rangers being at odds. Yosemite is crowded though; everything has to have a balance, and we have to share it. Gunnison was different, quiet and uncrowded; you kind of have to make friends with all types of people, from the rednecks to the cowboys to the liberals to the government official who is opening up the gate of a public land so that you can tow your broken down car to town.

I met him at the gate. He was dressed how all rangers are: tightly fitting gray clothes, a nametag, and a general appearance of organization and control. I showed up unkempt, unshowered, showing no organization or control—free as the wind blows.

It was awkward, but he didn't hate me. I didn't hate him. He was actually helping me. I was still worried about getting in trouble for the weed, but he didn't speak of it, so I didn't bring it up.

The tow truck driver arrived, and we all got in the truck. We spotted the car and hooked it up to the tow truck. Coming down Kill Hill, with fresh snow, packed into this massive truck, with a government ranger, we gently crawled down, and I had thought, *Only in Gunny*.

When I arrived back at the police station to prove I'd removed my car from Hartmans, I was nervous at the prospect that I would then be charged with the marijuana. But the secretary was nice, and she didn't say a word. I was off the hook. *Only in Gunny*, I thought again.

In late December, Two Tent and I finally got our act together and rented a house in Gunnison. We needed a third roommate and found her in the form of a coworker of mine, Amber. She was sweet and motherly and quickly earned the nickname *Mom*.

Our house was a classic college rental. The floor was crooked, so we named it the Crooked House. Compared to crashing out on friends' couches and floors, it was luxurious.

My first couple of winters, I stood in amazement of the stark white beauty of snow and mountains. But this winter, the climbing bug had me so bad I just wanted the cold weather to be over, so I could climb again. I fell into a sadness, a depression, but nothing that couldn't be cured with some friendship and the eventual return of spring. By this point I had too many friends to feel alone.

I lazily enrolled back in college, with only a few credits. I took an upper-level English class on Bob Dylan, something I thought I'd love because I love Dylan's greatest songs as much as I love climbing, nature, Colorado, and women. Problem was, the professor and I didn't see eye to eye. When I had a creative idea and he shot it down, I would become deflated. It was a far cry from the joy I felt writing alone next to the campfire with no one but God to see. In the beginning, I thought becoming a writer would be entirely fed by inspiration, not hard work. I stopped going to the Dylan class and forgot to drop it. When I received my transcripts, I saw an F in Bob Dylan 301.

My time living in the Crooked House was one of those periods that was formative yet unremarkable. I was lazy and wanted to do nothing but climb. Climbing is the perfect activity for a lazy fit person. To be lazy and climb full time is a crime of sorts; it's a gift to have the opportunity to live such a life; there are millions on this planet who work all day just to provide meager meals and housing for their families. The life of an American Climber is one of true privilege, for it does not take too much money, but it takes a juxtaposition of growing up middle class, so you are okay with living poorly, with the idea that someday you'll return to the middle-class lifestyle; it takes a liberal arts type of education to know that such a life is valuable, and it takes a community to make such a lifestyle alluring.

Townes Van Zandt wrote it best though: "Living's mostly wasting time," and sometimes you just waste and waste until you see the vision that every day is worth your best effort, but to give your best effort means you've found something that is your life's work. I had found it, but I didn't have the drive just yet. I was still just high on living the life of a dirtbag.

When I returned back to Illinois for the holidays that winter, I could only see two worlds: the places I lived and climbed and "back home." The Midwest and the cities of the United States were bleak; they were everything that was wrong with the world: polluted, crowded, and ugly.

I didn't yet see that we are all connected. The life in Gunnison is made possible by everything else in the world. We didn't grow our own food, or produce our own power; everything was provided by the intricate systems of energy and highways.

I just saw my own sadness, and it came out the most when I was in the flatlands. Had I stayed, I easily could have killed myself. I just sat around when I was back in Illinois and waited until the trip was over, so I could return to my true home. I was still a sad young man.

I also still had not found my way with women. Cherise left a mark on my heart that would be there forever; at least, that's how I thought then. I was also clueless on how to properly pursue women. In short, I had no game.

I was all about mixtapes and poetry. Yeah, we made mixtapes not even that long ago, kids. And I wrote poetry. I loved it, and I know in my heart that the poetry I wrote in those days was the purest writing I've ever done and will ever do. However, writing a poem to a woman in the first week that you're dating is not always appropriate. It scares them off, especially when there is a vibe of desperation in your delivery. Love is magic. Love is art. Love also learns from failure, and I had plenty of mistakes to make still.

Love comes from friendships too, and my new roommate Amber taught me a lot about love. She had a sad start to her adult life because her mother died. You could tell it still deeply affected her, and her life was defined by it. Amber also taught me about the greater world. She had made countless volunteer trips to Nicaragua to build houses and help the people there. It had clearly touched her soul, and she spoke of Nicaragua with great joy. They had even constructed a small concrete house for a family, in memory of her mother. I guess Amber became our mom because she realized how important her own mother was to her.

We lived somewhat similar to poor people as dirtbag climbers, but it was a poorness that was actually a luxury; almost every dirtbag climber I ever met was from the middle class. Grow up poor and you don't seek out to live poor; grow up rich, and it's the same.

While I was in a tent for four months, I started to learn about other dirtbag trickery. Hitchhiking was one tool in the box—put your thumb out and someone would always pick you up, at least in

Gunnison or Crested Butte. It may take an hour or two, and those two-hour waiting sessions built so much character that you were ready to throw away your character and give up your pride and go back to a normal way of living, but someone would always stop.

Couch surfing was like camping, yet you relied on the kindness of a friend or a stranger to provide that roof over your head; it was a delicate art form, riding a wave of timing and hospitality, for a place to crash.

Then there was dumpster diving. Could something be more dirtbag than dumpster diving? I learned about it from my friends Scott and Mark, two younger guys who arrived on the Gunnison climbing scene with a hunger and optimism that was impossible to ignore. I was just a couple years older, insignificant now, but, in college, two years was a lot; I met Scott when he cornered me in the college library, asking me everything about camping. He truly wanted to know *everything* about free camping, right then and there. That meant so much to me; I imparted all my knowledge in a quiet library voice. Just a couple years ago, I was that hungry kid, and now I had knowledge I could share. It felt divine, like a spirit sent me this guy, hungry and thirsty for dirtbag wisdom, and somehow I qualified because I was living the dream.

Scott and Mark started off dumpster diving for food, which has never really been my thing. They would uncover uneaten strawberries still in the package and try to share them with me. I declined, always, but I was fascinated that grocery stores throw away perfectly good food because of an expiration date. It wasn't just one package, it was often twenty packages, and they would devour those berries like a bear coming out of hibernation. Right then and there, I was witnessing the dirtbag future of America.

Once they uncovered sixty cans of beer in a dumpster, I started to take notice. Food that had sat next to other disgusting trash was one thing, but a can of beer? That was like finding gold. Then they would dumpster dive at the local thrift store and find layers of clothing that would keep them warm through the cold Gunnison winter.

I joined them in dumpster diving at the thrift stores. Every once in a while, we would find something very cool, brand-name fleeces and jackets that were perfectly fine to wear. My mind started turning—look at all the valuables America throws away? Why? Why do we have so much when others have so little? Even in our own country there were people that found value in what others throw away. One man gathers what another man spills, as the old saying goes. America's cup had runneth over.

My treasure hunt in the dumpsters of America culminated in finding money in the dumpster. I had a vision that someday I would find a twenty-dollar bill. First it started with a crumpled up dollar in a pocket of jeans, and then I found a five-dollar bill. A year after I had my vision, I reached into a pocket of pants that were delicately discarded, hovering at the top of a dumpster, and, what do you know, a fresh twenty-dollar bill.

I yelled it from the mountaintops and told every dirtbag I knew, with immense pride. I'm not a man of math or numbers, but I started to think, if I was finding money in a couple dumpsters in one of the quietest corners of America, just exactly how much money was thrown away every year? Had I been an accountant, like my father is, I would have created a spreadsheet and gave that number an estimate. Instead, I decided, once and for all, I would be a dirtbag, American climber, forever, and proclaim the joys of such a lifestyle to all who would listen. The cause would be righteous, and my karma would be right.

The biggest prize had yet to be claimed. Many moons after I found my twenty-dollar bill, my friend Lindsey, the dirtbag climber queen of Gunnison, from Illinois like myself, would be digging through that same dumpster. She found a ring. A diamond ring. A fucking diamond ring! *Could it be real*, she wondered? A tingle went down her spine. She took it to a local jeweler and had it appraised. It was real, and it was worth a thousand dollars. To a dirtbag, a thousand dollars is a lot of living. The lesson was worth more—in America, in our dumpsters, bound for a landfill, were prizes worth finding, scavenger hunts to discover valuables you could use to feed yourself with, to clothe yourself, and a pirate's treasure, booty, as they call it, to sell and fund a climbing trip.

Chapter 17

I was a lifestyle climber—that was for sure. My abilities quickly plateaued, and I celebrated the life and freedom more than my skills to attain a high level of climbing. In the beginning I wanted that, to reclaim something I'd never found in ball sports growing up in the Midwest. That quickly faded when I fell in love with the dirtbag life.

Winter was the best time to prove your love. Two Tent and I were so damn excited to climb, we headed out to the local crags at high noon, with hopes that the temperatures would lend themselves to a couple hours of decent temperatures. We were almost always wrong.

Taylor Canyon, a modest yet striving and striking granite canyon that forks off from Gunnison about twenty miles to the northeast, was the stage upon which our process of being molded into traditional climbers took place. To trad climb means to place your own gear; before sport climbing was invented, it was simply called rock climbing. I was glad I was already born into climbing after the dust had settled; sport climbing, bouldering, and gym climbing all came into popularity during or after the 1980s, and it all must have seemed shocking to the old school climbers, especially the hoards of people that were drawn to it. To be old school, to have climbed in the 1970s and before, all the way back to the ancestors who climbed rocks for necessity, meant that you were bold because the activity demanded it. Now, in modern times, you don't have to be brave to be a climber. With trad, you do still have to be brave, hence to be traditional means to take it back to the essence.

So we stood at the First Buttress of Taylor Canyon, the purple truck parked on the edge of a snowy parking lot. The First Buttress rises just over a couple hundred feet in the air, only a thirty-second hike from the parking lot, just close enough you could get yourself into trouble before even considering said trouble.

Snowy, dreamy, alpine, we forged through some snow to our objective. The air crisp, our hearts eager and foolish, we arrived at the base of a dihedral and racked up. I started leading, cleaning snow from the cracks with frozen hands, jamming upward.

I moved at a snail's pace, as Tim settled into a cold belay. It was terrifying not being able to feel my hands and then putting my feet on snowy edges and almost falling off. The worst part was crawling onto the belay ledge with a foot of snow. The whole time I thought I was going to slip off and fall down the ledgy climb and break an ankle or worse. Finally, I built a belay at that ledge and stood there in the snow. When Tim followed the pitch and joined my perch, we decided to rappel off.

Part of being a climber is realizing what kind of climber you are not. After throwing ourselves on snowy rock climbs in the middle of winter, Two Tent and I realized we were not destined for alpine climbing, for climbing high in the mountains in cold temperatures. Believing that I should try it all, I also attempted getting into ice climbing.

Again, like camping in the snow cave in the middle of winter, ice climbing was part of my curriculum for the recreation degree I was slowly earning. I'd been a handful of other times, and it seemed like a good thing to do to keep in shape for rock climbing.

Ouray just happened to be a mere two hours away, the little Switzerland of America—the ice climbing mecca of Colorado. A snowy, sleepy place, our sixteen-passenger van rolled in, full of college students, an instructor, and a couple teacher's assistants.

We organized and equipped ourselves with crampons and ice axes, ready for battle with ice. All day long, we climbed up the frozen waterfalls of Box Canyon; the actions of the day revolved around climbing and belaying one another, as well as calling out "ice" as inevitable chunks would come off and fall to the ground. A sport of impermanence, it's perfect for some who might like the essence of it.

I was on my last climb of the day, swinging my axe into the ice and gently kicking my crampons in, when I heard the most terrifying release. It sounded disastrous, like ten refrigerators sized blocks coming unglued from the wall and falling to the ground. The sound that followed that was worse—a man yelling and screaming at the top of his lungs.

It all sounded like something out of a horror movie. I made it to the top of the climb and just stood there while a rescue was formed. Our instructor, trained as a first responder, helped the victim. Our class stood at the bridge, horrified, seeing something we'd heard about, an accident, but assuming we'd never witness one.

A rescue truck arrived, and they hauled the injured climber out. Once our instructor was done helping, he joined the group and explained what had happened. A huge ice pillar had come undone, and a climber was standing directly underneath it. The pillar landed on his legs and snapped them in half, breaking his tibias and fibulas. I would have screamed bloody murder as well. And that was the end of my ice climbing days.

It's not to say rock climbing was completely safe, but I guess, in the end, you have to pick your poison. Nothing rewarding is without risk—even getting in a car is a major risk—but, as I was participating in these extreme mountain activities, I had a feeling I was perhaps choosing what I could die doing. I never wanted to die climbing, but, after those two near-death experiences I had, I knew I was so drawn to climbing that only death or severe injury would take me away from it; and though I was lousy at math, I knew enough that, if I did every sport that I could possibly die doing, the odds would be stacked too high. So ice climbing, for me, went the way of skiing, kayaking, and alpine climbing, something to save for another lifetime.

Chapter 18

Don't blame me I was given this world, I didn't make it

—*2Pac, "Keep Ya Head Up"*

My newfound undying optimism that I'd attained through climbing and mountain culture met with the grim realities that were painted in the larger picture of the state of the world. As a country, we were at war, and the more I studied, the more I learned about the woes of the world.

There are so many problems in the world, and there is so much access to information about such problems that it can make one feel hopeless and paralyzed to take action. The light that I'd felt—and wanted to bring more of into the world and my life—was held up high by Amber. The light of her life was Nicaragua. Amber was easily depressed, and her mother's death left a permanent mark on her soul, but, if you brought up Nicaragua and her time spent volunteering there, she lit up like the sun coming over a mountain crest.

I'd never really left the country, save for visiting a couple islands in the Caribbean on a cruise with my family, and so I decided to go and experience Nicaragua with Amber. I was joined by my friend Greg, who I met at work in the restaurant. On paper, Greg and I were nearly identical: both from Central Illinois with interests in climbing, hippie culture, and humanitarian causes. We both also spoke terrible Spanish and were equally naïve about the world.

Greg was one of several friends from a crew that I'd become friends with, not merely climbers, but also just hungry college kids in the mountains; they had formed their crew during freshman year, my first year in Gunnison, but I was not destined to meet them until their sophomore year; I was too sad anyways my first year. They were all optimistic; they could party till dawn and then still spend all day outdoors, skiing, biking, climbing, whatever you can name.

Greg and I spent months planning the trip with Amber. She would already be down there, and we would meet her. We decided to fly into Costa Rica and spend half our trip with Amber and the other half rambling around Costa Rica.

We got the cheapest tickets imaginable and thus had a layover in the airport in Houston. We set up a tent and slept in it, right there in the airport. It felt odd, as sleeping in an airport always does. Finally, we boarded our plane and were en route to the tropical land of Costa Rica. When we emerged out of the airport and onto the streets of San Jose, we truly were released into another world.

The young American, like myself, spends time dreaming and wondering about the places he'll go and how he'll find his way, and then, when he arrives, it's a feeling of fear because he really has no foundation of international travel, and he doesn't speak the language, and he's on his own. That was me, and that was Greg, and we were off on our first international adventure.

The streets of San Jose had a hustle and a bustle, and everywhere was Spanish we didn't understand and a general feel that this was a city unlike any we'd ever seen. By instinct, we found the bus station, bought a ticket to the border of Nicaragua, and waited. We waited for the bus to arrive and took it all in, hot, sweaty, and time had slowed down to a screeching halt, and we tried to put together the logistics. The distance between San Jose and Nicaragua seemed small on a map, but, once we got a feel for Costa Rica, we realized that our expectations for American-style travel were unrealistic.

With all the anticipation of the trip, all the planning, we were a bit surprised to find ourselves sitting like Buddha, waiting for the bus to the border to arrive. Finally, it did, and we boarded a bus that looked like it had been used in the United States for thirty years and then shipped down to Costa Rica, like an older brother's hand me downs. But, when the bus started moving, some romance came along with it, and we began to see the country.

The bus seemed to stop every ten minutes. We would talk to each other and worry about where we were staying that night, and then we would just sit and take it in. It was exciting. Pretty Costa Rican girls got on the bus. This was just a routine day in their lives I imagined, but it was exotic and otherworldly to us, their existence putting butterflies in my stomach. My Spanish was so bad I didn't dare try to talk to them. Greg and I barely even talked, just taking it all in. When we talked, we were worried about where we were going to stay that night. We kept worrying and worrying, until late in the night, dark, nearing midnight, the bus stopped at the border. We got out, and there was a feeling of history, of conflict—an industrial feeling of division.

Two wide-eyed and tired American kids fresh off the bus, with full backpacks of what we thought we should bring for three weeks of travel in Central America, we were surrounded by poor people offering us help. We just needed a place to crash for the night. At that point, I had the ability to sleep nearly anywhere. Greg was resilient too. One boy dragged us away from the hordes of people that seemingly wanted our help for some unidentifiable reason, spoken in Spanish. He offered us a place to stay for five dollars. We were weary and haggard and took the deal. Our hunger seemed to pale in comparison to the hunger of the twenty people we left outside.

Our sleeping quarters were extremely basic. The wall was covered with spider webs, and the door barely locked. Greg and I were scared. We locked the door as best we could and fell into a restless sleep.

In the morning, we crossed the border. It had a feeling of sketchiness; there were girls who looked like prostitutes, and that was sad. There were people just hanging around the border with eyes that seemed hungry and souls that seemed lost. We just needed to get a hundred miles north to Masaya. A young man approached us and offered to take us there by taxi. Fifteen bucks. All right, we said, naively. Greg and I got in the taxi and headed north.

On the radio came 1990s hip-hop songs. Long forgotten catchy pop tunes like, "Baby Got Back." We passed the lush, tropical countryside; there was minimal conversation, just the wind in our hair and the radio blasting words I'm sure the driver didn't understand.

'Cause I'm long, and I'm strong

And I'm down to get the friction on

So ladies (Yeah)

Ladies (Yeah)

If you wanna roll in my Mercedes (Yeah)

Then turn around, stick it out

Even white boys got to shout

Baby got back

Growing up in America, if you don't travel and roam the rest of the world, it's easy not to understand how much our culture influences the rest of the planet. Listening to Sir Mix-a-Lot and MC Hammer, as we traveled to our tropical destination, we were strangely comforted by American pop culture twenty years gone.

When we arrived in Masaya, Amber greeted us with a wide eyes and a grin and then told us how foolish we were. She said we should have taken a bus, and she was surprised we weren't robbed by the taxi guy. We just stood there, innocent, dumb white kids in another country, glad to be at our destination safe and sound.

Amber was our guardian; she spoke perfect Spanish and navigated situations to keep us fed and safe. We built a concrete house, with and for Nicaraguan people. One of the employees, a jovial heavyset guy, found out about our love for nineties hip-hop and recited Vanilla Ice's "Ice Ice Baby" daily. He danced and smiled, and we smiled.

These small concrete houses, built for families living in extreme simplicity, were so basic even two poets from a liberal arts college could take part in the construction. We mixed concrete, stacked the blocks, and took breaks to talk shit, eat snacks, and drink water. Chickens and pigs wandered the dirt roads of the neighborhood. Strange birds made Nintendo-like noises. Babies cried, music blasted, and this simple life was lived out in the open.

I got sick and lived life close to a toilet for a couple days. Greg and I played chess and wrote in our journals. At the end of a week filled with so much purpose, we set out to explore Nicaragua and Costa Rica.

More bus travel—always the slow bus travel, I realized, in Nicaragua. We went to Ometepe, an hourglass-shaped island that sits in the middle of a giant freshwater lake.

We were the only white people on a rowdy bus on a Friday night. I felt scared. I thought of our friend Adam, who had an appetite for travel and adventure far deeper than what I had at the time. He got robbed in South Africa at gunpoint and later told me, "It was so cool."

I thought of him when I felt vulnerable as we headed into the town where we would stay and climb a volcano. I realized I was not brave, and the world was a big place. But, nothing happened the Nica people just looked at us. What was I so afraid of? What do two young college kids have that's of much value anyways? A few dollars, a journal, some food.

We "climbed" the volcano—it was more like hiking. It was hiking. Challenging bushwhacking through thick groves of plants, but no adrenaline rush. At the top, we peered into a foggy, chilly chasm and looked out to the massive Lake Nicaragua. We stumbled down and celebrated with beer and Cuban cigars.

Then we bussed back to the Costa Rican border. We rambled through Costa, starting in a party town, where we stayed the night on the beach and woke up in the middle of the night to the tide slapping our tent. We wandered the beach and took naps at random locations until the sun came up.

In Costa Rica, I felt like a tourist; in Nicaragua, I felt like I contributed something during our visit. I hated that because travel should never merely be transactional. I never wanted to feel like a tourist in places where people had less than I did. It was a feeling I didn't like.

Travel through Costa Rica felt like a sleepy novelty. Why I

couldn't enjoy the horizontal more then was a mystery; I was ready for this trip to be over so I could climb. I was in a tropical paradise, rambling on the beach as a twenty-five-year-old, and all I could think about was getting back to the United States and scraping up some stupid rock.

In Montezuma, a little party town on the beach, there was a drunk man who sang opera in the streets at night; he seemed to have a little more status and dignity than your average bum. Mr. Table was his name. Bums are the lowest of the low in the United States, failures for all to see on the streets of the cities. In Costa Rica, it seemed a little more acceptable; maybe their social ladder did not extend so high into the sky as ours did.

One day in Montezuma, before we'd planned a big hike to a surf town, we played around at the local waterfall. Nothing huge, maybe thirty, forty feet, an idyllic setting, but serious enough that several memorials were there for those that had fatefully passed away in accidents. After sitting around and being lazy, I watched a local tico do his circuit, jumping from lower points and then higher and higher. At one point, I decided to join him. He climbed up on the fractured rock, using old twine that was tied into the rock for handholds. Compared to the climbing I'd been doing, this was insanely dangerous. I gave up following him when he reached the top and dove into water. But, I felt that adrenaline I'd become addicted to and called it a day.

That night, we decided to hike to Mal Pais, a surfing town. I wanted to wait until the next morning, but Greg insisted we charge into the night. Reluctantly, I agreed, and as we shouldered our packs, the night of the jungle was lit up by our headlamps, and we ventured into the unknown.

Greg was one of the people I could go into deep philosophical discussions with. We'd both rejected Christianity, we were both from Central Illinois, and we were both in love with the mountains. We felt disillusioned with the overall picture of things and envisioned a new world; the young man in post-industrial society, in love with the wild, always envisions a new way.

Greg wanted it all to fall to the ground, the military complex that rules the world. He envisioned peace, love, and happiness—that elusive state of being the hippies tried to cultivate in the sixties, and I guess some did. I wanted everything to be different, and we spoke to the wind passionately until we got tired and just had to keep hiking. We were tired and kept one foot in front of the other, wondering if we were lost; the brightest lights were the stars because there was no major town to see the lights of. Finally, we emerged, and, like all over Costa Rica, there was a little place to eat and drink beer. We found a place to stay and then spent the rest of the week surfing and being lazy in our cheap room we'd rented from a local family on the edge of the ocean.

We weren't really able to interact with the locals, and I felt completely like a tourist. I wanted to feel like we did in Nicaragua—part of something, helping out. Here I just felt like another transaction, a tourist that would come, eat, spend money, surf a few waves, and then there would be another gringo to replace me when I left.

We left early, and I think we were both homesick. We took a bus back toward San Jose and found a little pizza joint we'd previously stopped at—some of the best pizza I'd ever had. Two young American kids who were out in another country, searching for something, trying to save something; when, in retrospect, you're always searching for yourself, and the only person you can really save is yourself. You're never going to save the world, so we ended up eating pizza, and that made us happy.

We stayed in a cheap hotel by the pizza place and lazily watched TV. I'd misplaced the cheap, brown ditch weed, we'd bought, and there was no worse moment to have done that. Greg looked at me disappointingly; we were ready to go home.

In the San Jose airport, we played one last game of chess. I was teaching Greg to play on the trip, but, after fifty games, he had indeed learned everything I had to teach, and we were neck and neck. Somehow thirty Costa Rican people had surrounded us to watch the game. Oh, the great art of wasting time, some countries are built upon that, and, before the Industrial Revolution took hold of the world, was there really a notion that you could waste time? Like life has a playing clock, and your time is only valuable if you're accomplishing something, earning a paycheck and playing the game. I don't remember who won the game, only that great theater surrounding nothing really, just a couple of average chess players moving their pieces where they thought they should.

Arriving back home was the best part of the journey—at least it felt that way. I realized I didn't want to do another big trip that didn't involve climbing; at that time, it was not only my identity and my passion, it was my drug. I depended in the chemicals that climbing released for my happiness.

I rolled back into Gunnison, and again I was homeless. We'd just moved out of our apartment. I had to work the next morning; I'd become a climbing instructor with the college's outdoor program, paying back that good karma from the people who taught me how to climb. Plus, I was getting paid for it, and, at the time, I thought that was the greatest thing in the world.

I decided to sleep in the rolling sagebrush hills behind the college. By the light of the stars and my headlamp, I found a nice little place to lay down my sleeping bag—home for the night. I fell off into a deep sleep, figuring I would wake with the sun, and make it down just in time to guide.

I awoke to a feeling of someone grabbing my toes. I'd had a climbing mentor that always used to do that on early mornings, an easy way to wake someone up at 4:30 a.m. So in my half-awake, half-sleeping state of mind, I figured one of my friends had hiked up to wake me up. Then I looked up—it was a fox!

A fox was gently nibbling at my feet. Initially, I was a bit shocked and yelled at him, and he scurried off. As I rolled up my sleeping bag and headed onto campus for work, I should have thanked him. I was just in time to meet the dozen students that another guide and I were taking climbing.

Chapter 19

A few years into my life in Colorado, I was molded into a different person than I would have been if I'd stayed in Illinois. I became happy. Not every moment—Who among us is happy at every moment? —but I was grateful. I never cried a tear during the days I was severely depressed, in my parents' basement and driving aimlessly around trying to find Cherise, but, after the pain of those times subsided, the tears flowed.

Often, I'd be driving from Gunnison to my dishwashing job I'd taken in Crested Butte, and the beauty of the mountains would just hit me, and I'd realize how grateful I was for this life. How grateful that I'd survived a depression I thought I'd never escape without death. I cried because there was so much more in front of me that maybe I could have the life I wanted. I knew what I wanted, and it was simple: I wanted to climb, I wanted to find a woman to love, and I wanted to write. That was it. Tears of joy are a simple tonic, an elixir, a sign you're on the right path.

My path as a climber had to face a very real enemy: pure fear. This fear manifested itself in the biggest, baddest canyon, the most intimidating chasm in Colorado and even the entire United States—the Black Canyon.

The Black, as we called it, was basically in our backyard. Had it been farther away, I could have never faced it, never seen the terror or transcendence it has to offer. Since it was close, only an hour and a half away, there was no other option than to face it if you really wanted to call yourself a climber.

Two Tent dragged me up the first few routes I did in the canyon, and I simply held on, turning the lead over to him when I felt overwhelmed with fear. When we finished our climbs and had a couple celebratory beers over the rim, peering down and out at the two-thousand-foot walls, only then did I feel at ease, like I'd escaped, a prisoner of fear, climbing the wall to freedom.

Like a punch-drunk boxer, a climber returns to the Black. By now, Two Tent had fallen in love with a hippie girl he met at a concert, and they moved farther west to Oregon. I missed my best friend, but his absence gave me an opportunity to grow in my climbing. No longer could I reach out to his proverbial hand to get higher. I had to reach that place myself.

My buddy Dave, who we gave the nickname *5.14 Gene* after a Halloween outfit he wore so perfectly one year, a brightly colored spandex getup from the '80s—had the enthusiasm of ten climbers. One day, when I proposed that we should do a big climb in the Black, called The Cruise, he was on board with no hesitation.

The Black was already in my heart and soul, and it terrified me as much as it inspired me. There was a deep focus you could attain after toiling on the wall all day, and it was that focus, coupled with the chemicals that properly facing fear releases, that kept me coming back.

Whenever I would travel and tell climbers that I was from Gunnison, nearly every time they would look at me sideways and ask if I climbed in the Black Canyon. Its reputation preceded itself, an aura of fear, runouts, loose rock, and poison ivy. Some of my friends would confirm all those rumors and tell people it was basically a pile of shit and not worth visiting; they were afraid it would become popular and crowded. I never felt that way; I felt the aura and environment would naturally force people away. More than anything, more than any other climbing area, there was an aura about the Black.

It could be the suicides. More people die from suicide than climbing, exponentially, in the Black. Was it their spirits that haunted the inside of this chasm, this giant gaping hole in the earth? Was that why I could never sleep properly in the campground before the next day's climb? I've heard that the ancient people, the Utes, the inhabitants of the land before the white man came along, believed the canyon was haunted as well. But, I am not a religious man, nor a superstitious man, and I don't try to come up with answers to the big questions—I'm just here. And, when I was there, in the throes of the battle with mind and body, climbing a steep pitch of pegmatite split granite, I felt more alive, more in the moment, and clearer than at any point in my existence.

We arrived at night, too late, drinking Red Bulls on our drive and smoking weed. We were late because we watched the World Series; Gene, a child of the East Coast, was rooting for his Red Sox, so I obliged and watched with him. I don't recall if they won or lost. I do, however, remember this climb of The Cruise.

We awoke in darkness after fitfully tossing and turning for a few hours, so, basically, there was no solid sleep. Sleep is the magic ingredient for life, as far as I'm concerned, and I don't operate well without it. At this point in my climbing, I wanted to test myself. Sure, I was a lifestyle climber, but I wanted to grow. I wanted to prove myself. Not for recognition, but for inner growth. The tests that the Black Canyon offered were more memorable and more valuable than anything higher education presented in the classroom.

So Gene and I woke up, ate oatmeal, slammed coffee, pooped, and shouldered the ropes and gear as we slipped into a gully of poison ivy and fear. The sun came up as we found the base of the route. We were already fatigued and tired, and, had we known the angle of repose that an experienced climber has, we would have suggested something smaller, easier. That said, a climber can only gain experience through experiences. Everything else is just bullshit, talk, and the world has enough of that.

We looked at each other with the eyes of eternity before we started up. Gene led the first part, a wandering, fractured slab that leads to the base of a giant, wide crack. As I belayed and looked up, the wall in front of us seemed infinite; the top was so far away, I couldn't conceptualize that there could even be an end in sight. And these are the greatest climbs, when one is fully engaged with the experience, having no idea how it will turn out.

The off-width wide crack was my lead. I wanted it but only in the concept of an idea. The actual climbing of the crack was part horror, part beauty. The crack, wide enough to get my elbows and knees in, made me work for it. The Gunnison River lazily roared below, and soon my voice would be muffled; we would only communicate in the brotherhood of the rope; when I would pull up the rope to clip, Gene would know exactly what I was doing. When I ran out of rope and pulled it tight to Gene, he would have to start climbing. Two figure-8 knots together, two knots of eternity on each end of a ropelegth.

Jamming my elbows and knees in, in fear, a simple math equation, a puzzle demanded athleticism and the management of the mind. I was also climbing like an amateur, and, even though I had some Black Canyon climbs under my belt, I still fumbled and made movements like a scared beginner. I wore a small pack, filled with a hydration bladder and snacks for the climb, pears and some lemon bars my girlfriend had made.

As I was a hundred feet from Gene, my body slammed into the crack, I felt a sensation of water dripping down my back. The hydration bladder had leaked, and it dripped all the way down to my feet. I tried to move upward, but my shoes were covered in water. I didn't have a piece of gear in for twenty feet, and I panicked. My heart beat faster than it ever had in my entire life. Relax. Breathe. These are rarely followed but useful mantras in everyday life. In climbing, a simple mantra can keep you alive. *The fear is always greater than anything else*, you tell yourself. *Just breathe—you can get through this.*

I took my hand, put chalk on it, and rubbed the chalk on my feet. I prayed to God. I talked to myself like a drunken fool. I finally gained my composure, continuing upward progress until the rope got tight. I was still thirty feet from the next belay ledge and had no more rope. Gene would be forced to start climbing, not knowing whether or not he was on belay. He wasn't. I went into survival mode and moved, inch-by-inch, off-width climbing, one of the slowest forms of movement known to man.

I pulled up to the belay ledge and felt like I was going to puke. It took me hours to climb that pitch. I was humbled, hungry, hobbled, a mess of a man, and we still had a thousand feet of granite above us.

Gene led the crux pitch, a dihedral that lasted a rope length, delicately dancing up on dime-sized edges, placing gear when he could and running it out when he couldn't. I was amazed at his skill and didn't know if I could have led that pitch. I climbed slow and desperate, already exhausted in the autumn sun.

The next pitch was my lead. It was a gently overhanging dihedral with good holds. I grasped for them and my forearms failed me, cramping, unable to perform the basic task of holding on. I told Gene to lower me back to the belay. He did. I was wasting precious time, but to mention it would have been to waste more time. Gene was in better shape than I was and went up to take care of business. He did, but the sun was fading.

I led up and got off route, wandering up a granite slab to nowhere and then climbing back down. We were barely halfway up the wall and had only an hour of daylight left. I finally got on route and made a belay at the base of a massive flake. When Gene reached my perch, the sun had set. We had several pitches to go, probably seven hundred feet, and talked it out. We were both so exhausted we couldn't bear to continue in the darkness. We didn't want to go down because we would have to leave all our pieces as anchors, hundreds of dollars in gear, our most valuable and important possessions.

So we hunkered down, our first benightment. Time stopped, and a great darkness overcame us. It finally happened—an epic mistake of inefficiency. It was not like some climbing mistakes though; all we had to face was suffering at the moment, not injury or death. Sure, you could die in a benightment, if weather moved in and you or your partner became wet and hypothermic, but the stark clear sky suggested that that would not happen. We just had to suffer.

And we did. We didn't speak for a while, not out of anger toward one another, but for indifference at the situation. We were supposed to be celebrating on the rim, with the darkness below, but instead we drank nothing—our water was gone, and we were one with the darkness.

The ledge was just enough to sit upon, nothing else. We started to shiver and huddled together, wrapping the rope around us for some protection. We were too cold and uncomfortable to sleep. An eternity went by, and then another eternity. We checked our watch for time and were always disappointed.

We talked about what we wanted. We wanted food and water and a woman to hold for warmth. We rubbed each other's shoulders, trying to keep warm. We were cold, on the verge of dangerous cold. I thought of my girlfriend, Christina. I longed to hold her tight. She was my first real girlfriend since Cherise. She picked me up hitchhiking one day from Gunnison to Crested Butte, but it wasn't until a year later that I would run into her again. She was the first person I'd told *my story* to. I'd always felt ashamed and embarrassed. She understood, and, upon telling the story, I was a little freer. Unchained. Before telling her in my bedroom one night, I felt a tremendous fear, but it was an imagined fear—she didn't like me any less, and maybe she felt that me telling her brought us closer together. Why does depression make us feel so alone?

In the middle of the night, Gene dropped his headlamp. It fell twenty feet down in the rock, and we could see it, but there was no way we would get it. Somehow I'd packed an extra, tiny headlamp that he could use for the rest of the night.

We waited and waited, and lifetimes seemed to pass by. When that sun hit us, it was the most glorious feeling in the world. We greeted the sun as our God. It blessed us with warmth, and we forced ourselves to soldier on. Climbing should be like this, I knew then and forever. For you should have to suffer for your dreams. You should have to prove to your dreams that you are worthy. Some dreams, like climbing dreams, often demand lives; they demand that young men and women are killed in their prime; such dangerous dreams do we have as climbers.

On day one, I was the weak link. I took too long on my leads and was unable to perform on others. On day two, I had some chance at redemption. Gene was feeling extremely dehydrated and requested that I lead. I obliged, and I felt like I was climbing for the both of us; you are always in a partnership, but this day felt different—this felt like survival climbing, which I guess the activity of climbing has its roots in survival.

The second lead of the day involved a traverse with over a thousand feet of air beneath my shoes I was feeling it out, discovering how the holds felt and the best way to lean into them. On these leads, I think I discovered that I was truly a climber because I didn't hate it. So much had gone wrong; we were out of food and water, and my body felt terrible. But, in this movement upward for survival, somehow there was a great, divine purpose.

Gene felt worse and worse and was depending on me more, which somehow made me feel better. We moved at a snail's pace up the wall as it became more and more fractured near the top. And, finally, it was over.

We craved water more than anything. Then we drank the sky. It was so blue, and we felt so blessed to be alive. It was a privilege to suffer. We knew that then. Soon, I had what we wished we had more than anything in the world while freezing and starving on that ledge throughout the night: food, water, and a woman.

That night I held Christina tightly. Under the cover of blankets and love, a journey had been completed, and the magic of the Black Canyon was alive in my heart.

Chapter 20

True climbing encourages bravery and induces suffering. It's at the heart of the endeavor, and all seasoned climbers recognize this. For most of us it creates a foundation of who we are, builds our character, and gives us life philosophies. For most of time, climbing was never mainstream. Then, starting with sport climbing, gyms, and bouldering, climbing reached more and more people. It reached me as a hopeless kid growing up in the flatlands.

Fortunately, I landed in Gunnison, where a hierarchy in the climbing culture was basically nonexistent. That's a good thing. All climbers being created equal. Sure, we're not equal in terms of ability, but no one was going to think or act like they were better than you simply because they climbed higher and harder. There was a spiritual flare to it, and that is what appealed to me the most. The greater climbing scene could be weird. Climbing, no matter how mainstream it gets, will always have the weirdos—good or bad.

Visit any crowded climbing area, and you're bound to find some weird. The current state of climbing is a sport trying to find its identity. All hope is not lost though; once you become a competent climber, you realize there's an abundance of rock on which to paint your art. At least in the American West and especially where we were at in these days. Climbing at its core, a dirtbag sport, rejects the mainstream. But climbing is mainstream nowadays, and we're still sorting it all out.

Ancient Art, located in the heart of the Utah desert, in the Fisher Towers, is one of the most photographed summits in the desert—an iconic corkscrew that winds up into the blue sky, having an unbalanced summit with room enough for only one person. It is disgustingly crowded on a busy weekend, and a testament that often, as a whole, the climbing community lacks vision and skill; why in the world we will climb behind ten other people says something about the modern human race.

Ancient Art is no Mount Everest though; people aren't dying regularly because of the problems. It's simply an inconvenience. And, when we were in our younger twenties, we saw no problem getting behind several parties and starting up.

It was Two Tent, Tim and I leisurely climbing the Stolen Chimney behind several other parties. We were far from wise—no young climber is ever wise—but we were willing to climb slowly, and we really wanted to stand on that corkscrew summit.

So we waited behind the line, and, eventually, after an hour, it was our turn to start up. Two Tent led the first part, and he was like a Zen machine; you knew he would get the job done with ease and style. I belayed and simply fed out rope as he motored up the pitch. As he finished, and built the belay, a character emerged out of nowhere. "Hey, you guys mind if I pass you?" he asked.

Slightly stoned, we were already laughing about an incident that had just happened, when one of the parties rappelled down and dropped a rope on a climber coming up. The woman started freaking out, yelling, "I'm down here. I'm down here," as if certain death and doom were going to follow the rappel ropes.

So we were laughing and stoned, and okay with everything, until this guy showed up. First of all, it was just him. He had no partner, and he wanted to rope solo the route. Rope soloing is an art of the 1 percent in climbing, probably less than 1 percent. I've met a few, and their prime seemed to be in their mid to late twenties; and they were going through a breakup or some identity crisis. They needed to prove who they were to themselves. The Fisher Towers, the Black Canyon, and Yosemite have witnessed some impressive and partially insane rope solos; pushing the limits with a partner is one thing, but pushing those same limits with no one but yourself to be your best friend is another.

I doubt this guy was one of the proud ones; my guess is that he was so annoying he had a hard time finding steady partners. So that fateful day, his motivation to climb with no partner, put him behind us and ten other people.

"I don't know," I said to the guy, while looking at Tim. "I think we'll probably move faster than you. You have to climb each pitch twice, man."

He was unfazed and motivated to shoot to the top of the tower in the fastest possible time. Two Tent built an anchor, and we climbed up to the ledge. Then we sent Tim up. Tim was just in his first year of leading and moved slowly, as one often does when learning. He was in a chimney and kept climbing farther and farther into it for security. Solo Guy came up and forcefully built his anchor, using the same bolts we were clipped to. He quickly rappelled down and cleaned all of his gear, moving efficiently, but still annoyingly.

When he was back up at our ledge, Tim was still deep in the chimney, moving slowly. Fear and lack of experience can make time stand still for the leader, gripped, thinking injury may be one move away. With Solo Guy back at our anchor, Two Tent and I were just laughing at his presence when he announced that he can't stand it anymore—he's climbing.

Tired of his company, we just let him go, and he started up the chimney, with Tim forty feet above him. He quickly climbed to Tim, and they talked. Solo Guy was spread eagle on the outside of the chimney, with Tim deeper in the chimney. "You see, your first problem is your pants," Solo Guy said. "They're too baggy; you need to get something that fits better."

We're laughing quietly to ourselves at the belay. Tim was frightened and we didn't want to upset his nerves, and we also didn't want Solo Guy to know we're making fun of him. Two Tent and I were in a world of safety, beauty, and camaraderie; Tim was scared, and perhaps learning something about pants and climbing, and Solo Guy was fired up to pass as many parties as possible to stand alone on the corkscrew summit of Ancient Art.

Solo Guy passed Tim, awkwardly climbing the chimney spread eagled, and he's still giving advice, and now addressing Tim like he's his best friend and mentor. "Hey, Tim, I don't mind if you clip my gear, but if you clip this one you might die."

Two Tent and I stared at each other, lost in the comedy.

"This one is okay though; you can clip it," Solo Guy said.

Solo Guy finally left our sight, and Tim slowly climbed up. Then

Solo Guy came down to clean his gear, giving more advice to Tim, and then he went back up. Tim and him arrived at the next anchor near the same time. He brought us up.

We arrived at the ledge only to look up to Solo Guy passing more parties, surely annoying others as much as he annoyed us. At the ledge, we had more company—a guy and a girl, the girl being the one who was frantically yelling earlier.

Here's another phenomenon in the modern climbing world: guy learns to climb, guy wants to impress girl, guy takes girl climbing, guy is unsafe and gets girl in over her head, girl has meltdown, fighting ensues and echoes throughout the climbing area for all to hear. This was one of those situations.

I could imagine a scenario where the roles were reversed, but the old saying—"the women are smarter"—speaks for itself. Most of us are still cavemen.

We introduced ourselves, and so did they. They rappelled back to the ground, and we had a second of solitude. The main feature unfolded before us on the last pitch, a small walkway, a diving board's width, leading up to a thirty-foot corkscrew-looking feature, winding around to the summit. A thousand feet of air beneath you and the classic red rock Old West desert landscape, but this is the new West.

Climbing on the feature, it seems like something that's going to fall down one day, destined to be a part of the boulders and bushes and trees below. Probably would scare the shit out of some rabbit frantically running about on the desert floor for food, safety, or sex. The phrase "fucking like rabbits" is said all the time, but, in all my days in the wild, I've yet to see it. Maybe I'm just not looking at the right time. Maybe the rabbits are more discreet than we give them credit for.

Back up at a thousand feet, we finally had the tower to ourselves. Two Tent led, weaving the rope up the corkscrew formation like a spider, carefully, with ease. He stood on top, and, when he stood on top, he looked comfortable. When I went up on toprope, I stood on top and immediately climbed back down. The top was slanted, and I felt like any sudden movement meant either I was going to fall off, or the tower was going to fall down. And, what if it did? Would I survive? Would I be "that guy who was on Ancient Art when it fell down?" It didn't. It still stands to this day, although, just last year, The Cobra, an often climbed shorter tower in the Fishers did just that—it fell to the ground.

No word on rabbit fatalities.

Two Tent, Tim, and I, the ninth, tenth, and eleventh people to stand on that little guy that day, rappelled back to the ground, only to find eight more people, lined up like they were at Disney World.

A couple seasons later, Tim and I returned with Jerid to repeat the climb. It was slightly less crowded, no rope soloists in sight either. At the diving board feature, on the way to the summit, we made fun of Jerid while he humped across it, beached whale style, trying to take a photo of him. He jokingly swiped for the camera, a disposable one (still predigital camera era here), and it fell out of Tim's hands. We watched the thing fall a thousand feet, like a slow motion movie, slowly, slowly falling back to the desert floor.

Bummed that we would be losing some shots from a great trip, we tried in vein to find the camera as we hiked back down the trail. Tim became convinced that someone else had picked up the camera, and he ran down a family who was hiking. He was gone for twenty minutes, so we just sat there, blazing in the desert sun, ready for Tim to come back, so we could go drink beer and eat peanut butter and jelly sandwiches. Then, we saw him, on the horizon, hands in the air, "I found the camera!"

It was a glorious moment, and, when I took the camera in to process the photos—it was still relatively intact even though it fell a thousand feet—what do you know, the very last photo, the family had taken a photo of their kid, sunglasses tilted, hat brim leaning to the left, posing like a hip-hopper; the photo before that was Jerid, humping along the diving board, that delicate little summit behind him.

Chapter 21

When the days you dream about arrive, it's often different than you imagined. Graduating from college was spent in a daze of alcohol and celebration. I made a foolish speech at the dinner party following, and, that night, I cuddled up with a toilet, puking, a hellish experience that began a Dark Ages of sorts; I had to come of age again.

All I wanted to be was a climber. I knew I liked to write as well, but I lacked the discipline that a writer needs. When I would write, I would bask in the glory of a published article for far too long. I graduated college and wanted to be a climbing bum. That much I knew.

I went back to Yosemite, with the thought that perhaps I could live there and just climb. Surviving as a dirtbag climber there took too much energy. Rest days were spent selling aluminum cans for money and developing schemes to avoid the authorities. I didn't want to hide out in the boulders because of rangers and bears. I was woken up in the middle of the night in Camp 4 by rangers and bears more than once. On a rest day, we went to San Francisco. We stood at Haight and Ashbury, where the hippie movement that shaped my life so much began. I felt nothing. We returned to Yosemite.

One day, we were taking it easy and smoking weed in the boulder fields behind Camp 4. A ranger smelled the weed and approached us. "What are you doing back here?" she said, startling us.

"Um, nothing…" I nervously replied, while hiding the bag of weed in the palm of my hand, and, at the same time, sliding the pipe under some leaves.

"It smells like you're smoking marijuana," the ranger said authoritatively. "Now, where is it?"

"I don't know what you're talking about. He was smoking a cigarette, maybe it's that," I lied.

"C'mon, you guys, this is going to be easier if you just give me the weed and we can take care of this," she countered.

Now how in the world this ranger never discovered that weed, I'll never know, but I talked to her with my hand closed, hiding a meager amount of marijuana in my palm. My heart beat like a thundering drum, but I was not backing down. I couldn't start my post-college life with getting in trouble for pot in a National Park. We went back and forth for ten minutes, and I held my ground, my buddy sitting there doing the same. Finally, she asked for our licenses. She noticed we were from Gunnison.

"Oh, you're from Gunnison," she said excitedly. "That's where I went to college! Do you know Jimmy Dunn?"

"Well, we've heard of him, of course, but never met him," I said cautiously, surprised by her change of tone.

"What about Jimmy Newberry or Jim Nigro?" she asked. (Apparently all the great climbers of the 1970s in Gunnison were named Jim.)

"Uh, yeah, actually we do," I said, starting to think we had a way out of this.

"And, Tom Pulaski…"

"Yeah, we know him."

We did. He was our friend's landlord. All of a sudden, at the mention of some old school names, we had a *Get Out of Jail Free Card*.

This ranger was no longer the authority for the United States government; she was our friend. All because we knew some of the same people in this little, forgotten corner of Colorado.

"Okay, guys," she said in a friendly tone. "I'm going to run your licenses, and, if your records are clean, you're free to go."

Our records were clean. We narrowly escaped. I returned to Colorado with another Yosemite trip under my belt but with little direction in life. Fortunately, it was summer and, having ambition only to climb rocks and work a little to get by, that was simply enough. So that is what I did.

I lived out of my truck that summer. In the winter, I moved into an apartment. That winter, with school done and no focus, I felt lost and depressed. We went to Mexico, to Potrero Chico, the famous limestone sport climbing area. It opened up another part of the world, another part of dreaming. I decided I would never spend another winter in Gunnison and that I would only live there when it was warm, and I would travel North America to seek warm rocks during the long Gunny winters. But that led me back to my parents' house in Illinois after one Christmas, and I was forced to sit with myself and really think about who I was and where I was going.

Chapter 22

If you go down to the gas-powered flatland

Where most of the people just think

That they're free

Remember the peace that you had

On the mountain

—*New Riders of the Purple Sage, "Last Lonely Eagle"*

I lived in my parents' basement and got a short-time gig at a paper factory. I would save my pennies and head back to Mexico. At some point in a climber's life, the highs end, and you're forced to sit with yourself. What do you truly have, and where do you go from here? Since the climber collects memories and experiences, he often has little to show. I could fit everything I owned into my truck. Relationships with women were short; they were only around for summer vacation, or I would leave on a road trip. Was I truly happy with this life? I was incomplete, I realized, but I still wanted to chase those highs.

At the paper factory, I worked a night shift for minimum wage. It was incredibly humbling, but it was temporary. I knew I would not be doing this for the rest of my life. Rather, I'd only do it for a few weeks. I was living rent free at my parents', and I would be taking the money to Mexico, where it would sustain me for a reasonable amount of time. There were so many others working there to simply live, hand to mouth.

I knew I was a writer then, and I knew the writer has to observe to get away from a comfortable existence and just sit and absorb like a sponge. These people in the paper factory were dirt poor. I remember one guy from the other side of the tracks, the lower-class side that I certainly did not grow up in. Even in the moment, I knew I'd appreciate these days when I went to work and put paper in a box. I realized there are millions of people in the world that go to work every day in factories, and most people probably make the best of it. So many things we use in the modern world have to be assembled in a factory, and I assumed it was my part to pay my dues. I knew I believed in karma and the truths of it. Plus, I had nothing else going for me. I wasn't savvy enough to get much freelance writing work. I wasn't seeking a career; I just wanted enough money to climb for a month or two. That was all that mattered.

The nights I wasn't working, I would write. I had the delusion that I could write my great American novel. I just started. No outline, no plan, I just started right into it, and eventually fell into a wall. Thousands of words, and the idea just vanished into the air. *Fuck, man, the life of a writer is like this?* I wondered to myself.

The Illinois winter was flat and white and cold. I longed for kicks and reconnected with high school friends to go to the bar with. There was nothing worth chasing in my hometown though. Nothing for me other than shifts at the factory that would eventually give me enough money to leave.

I didn't tell any of my coworkers at the factory that I was a writer, not that anyone would have really cared. I realized it's a luxury to have dreams sometimes, because certain needs have to be met to have dreams. And to write was certainly a dream; I was lacking the structure and experience to write a book yet.

But I'd experienced magical states of transcendence before, when I recalled a great moment outside, or when I told the story of a specific adventure, and I knew I would continue to chase that dream. I don't know what other employees' dreams were. One Mexican kid told me about his path to the United States, and I told him I was saving money to go to Mexico, and he seemed to respect that. He was probably building a foundation so that he could dream, or maybe so his kids could dream. Getting by is hardly enough for the hungry soul. One poor black guy was talking with his other coworkers one day, and he was talking about his cousin, who was getting into trouble with simple sinning like smoking weed and such. "And she's eating those expensive seven-dollar sandwiches," he said. I knew, in that moment, I'd never forget those words. And I knew that I had a tremendous luxury in this life to want to be a climbing bum.

Another kid, who was Amish, was a terrible alcoholic. I just let him talk because I was a writer, and I would just study people and their odd intricacies. He said he started smoking cigarettes when he was nine and drinking when he was ten. His thing was building barns. "I got ten barns," he said. "Built them all."

He was sad. "My kid's gonna start smoking here soon; he's six now. I'll have him drinking too. Same way I did."

Damn, the saddest thing in the world is being so close to things that could make you truly happy, but choosing a life of smoke and drink, with little hope for greater pleasures. I wonder if my man ever worked his way up in the paper factory to afford those seven-dollar sandwiches? Or how many barns the Amish guy built, and when he inflicted his son with the same sadness and sickness he had? Or if my Mexican homey built a life for himself and his family here in the States? I knew I would never know. All I knew was I had to follow my dreams, because I could, and I would.

Chapter 23

After working in the paper factory and failing at my first attempt to write a book, I packed up my truck and headed to Mexico. A Craigslist hitchhiker came along, and we split gas, and he was terribly quiet and confused and seemed to be addicted to something, maybe heroin? All my life I've been shown the worst result, the saddest possible outcome, and I was somewhere in the middle. I wasn't hopelessly addicted to anything too strong; I smoked pot a little and drank a couple beers a night and more than a couple when we really partied, but I was spared from the curse of deep addiction and the darkness of all that. I dropped the hitchhiker off in Austin, Texas, visited some old college friends there for a couple days, and then drove into Mexico.

I was terribly nervous to drive all by myself into Mexico. Ironically, the Border Patrol in Mexico put me at ease when he casually did a search of my truck. He looked into a first aid kit and joked, "Coca, cocaine?" with that smile and tranquillo spirit that most Mexicans seem to have.

I passed through the sketchy border town, and, just a couple hours later, I was in El Potrero Chico. I met Scott there, my dumpster-diving amigo from college. He was on a grand tour of the climbing areas of the world, from South America to Thailand. His motivation was sky high, and, immediately after I arrived, he insisted we plan out our entire month together.

The life was as simple as my time at home with my parents and in the paper factory, but the joys were much more divine; we lived on just a few dollars a day and subsisted on the simple diet of Mexico: beans, rice, cheese, avocados, salsa, and sugary snacks when we were climbing. Cheap beers some nights. Sleeping in tents under the stars at the little places that Mexicans rent out to gringos like us for three dollars a night.

The simplest life I could imagine brought me the most joy. Since I didn't really have a home, I wasn't homesick. We would meet other climbers and try to surround ourselves with the ones who had the best vibes and attitudes. Negativity is a curse for a climber.

The town of Hidalgo, on the edge of Potrero Chico, is a simple place. There's a concrete factory, and the people there seem to move at a slow pace. They smile and wave to you when you go by, call you *guero*, which means blondie, and, even if you aren't really blond, they still call you that because you're a gringo. There's a market once a week where you buy your food, and they sell everything imaginable, and it's great to just people watch and realize how different things are there compared to back home.

And the cliffs, they simply blow you away at first, gray limestone walls towering up two thousand feet in the sky. Palm trees and cactuses growing from the walls. And your purpose in life is to sustain yourself, keep yourself healthy, and climb these walls until you must return home.

Sport climbing is rooted in routine and consistency. All of the routes in Potrero are bolted, a systematic difference from all of the other multipitch climbing I'd done in the States. Ethically, it was the complete opposite of our home walls near Gunnison, like the Black Canyon. It had to be. The gear in most limestone cracks is usually worthless, so you must have the bolts. Thus, the heightened awareness of traditional climbing is not needed there, at least not when the bolts are close together.

Naturally, catering to my ADD, I recall the driving as much as the climbing, which is probably ten times as dangerous and way less intuitive. We'd climbed at Potrero for two weeks and wanted some more adventure. We heard about an area called El Salto, which was on the other side of Monterrey, the second largest city in Mexico, located just less than an hour from Potrero. Still in an era before smartphones here, our directions were from a Mexican climber, who spoke broken English. My Spanish couldn't even be called broken—I was basically a two-year-old at speaking Spanish. Scott was better, and he always did the talking when we were out in public.

So there we were, in the kitchen of the hostel-like place where we were staying, getting directions scribbled out onto a piece of paper. And the directions had little information about roads or highways—once we got out of Monterrey, he was saying, "Look for the furniture store on the right; it will be closed. Keep going four miles past the furniture store until you see a series of Jesus statues for sale; this is where you make your next turn..."

Getting to the hillsides, the countryside where El Salto was, involved driving through the madness that is a big Mexican city. The shoulders are not shoulders there—they are another lane. God forbid anyone ever tried to ride a road bike there; they would be run over in minutes. To this day, I don't know how we made it, but we did; we drove past all the landmarks that our Mexican friend suggested, and we found El Salto, way out in the hills.

It was a magical place, just past a town with no phones or Internet but everything you needed to survive a few days. We subsisted on beans, rice, avocados, and cheese and climbed sport routes. The canyon had countless thousand-foot walls, but little development other than two crags that had overhanging sport routes. The walls were trippy, tufas that looked like mushrooms, a psychedelic vibe, and a feeling of punishment. All the climbs were above our heads, and we fell, tried again, and fell many more times. We camped in a wash, with no one else except a Canadian party, who were there to experience the same thing we were there to experience. We climbed until our forearms were worthless, and then we reversed our path back to Potrero Chico.

Our last day in Potrero, we decided to go big; for me, climbing doesn't feel right until you give it your all. So we decided to do three routes in a day. Everything went great; it was just pure movement over stone, followed by rappelling the climb to get back to where you started. Two thousand feet and twenty rappels into the day, we were on cruise control, fatigued from the climbing and subsisting on nothing but sugary Mexican snacks, when darkness overcame us. Scott was about sixty feet below me at a rappel station when I heard him calmly shout, "Hey...so there's a rattlesnake down here...a baby rattlesnake. It just rattled at me."

He spoke so calmly that it made me feel calm. I knew that baby rattlesnakes possess the most venom of all, and I knew that if Scott were to get bitten, logistically, it would have been a nightmare for him to get the necessary care. However, my happiness and my fatigue coupled with Scott's calm didn't reveal the seriousness of the situation.

Scott rappelled past the rattler, without incident, and then I had to go down. Blessed with the ignorance of the night, I didn't see the little guy, and I made it safely to the next rappel anchor. That night we celebrated our big day, with one big beer, a *caguama*, and a proper meal.

The next morning, I was filled with satisfaction, filled with the feeling that I couldn't climb that day even if I wanted to. I know a lot of my so-called ADD is channeled into climbing; my angst can be dissipated. There was little time to savor it though; Scott was headed to the airport that afternoon for Thailand, and I was headed back to the States.

Chapter 24

I have to admit that I was chasing the climbing high. I wanted to feel that feeling frequently and often, and I drove all over to find it. With any highs, there are the lows. Being a dirtbag climber, it's the loneliness of the road, at least for me; we all have our own demons. I was riding high out of Mexico, back into Texas, but the flat roads of Texas and Oklahoma had a way of killing the high.

Of course, I just had to find the next high. I stopped off in Gunnison, and it was still in the throes of winter. Gunny couldn't provide me with the fix I needed. So I kept moving, kept pumping gas into the truck, and ended up in the Utah desert. I climbed in Indian Creek for a while and then had the appetite for something bigger. Zion was the destination, a sandstone Yosemite of sorts; the kind of place that would feed my dreams and give me the fix I needed.

I'd lined up an old college buddy, Dave, as my partner. Dave was the ying to my yang—he was calm and collected, and I was a bit hungry and charged. After two months of mostly predictable climbing, I knew the tall walls of Zion would provide adventure. Dave was a climbing guide and had the demeanor; in many ways, he was the only truly experienced climber in our duo; he could read the weather and the rock and knew when to push onward and when to back off.

This was perfect because I was ready to just set sail in any type of weather; I just craved the adventure, and I was full of the hopeful, youthful enthusiasm that will get you into trouble quickly. And, when we were two pitches up The Touchstone Wall, a classic thousand-foot route of seams and cracks, a wicked storm started brewing above us. A towering wall of dark gray clouds hovered, but I still wanted to press on. Dave looked at me like I was a damn fool, which I was, and told me we needed to rappel down, right now. And we did, and the rainstorm ensued, keeping the sandstone wet for days, so we rolled around the area in my truck, just wasting time.

The area surrounding Zion is a Mormon stronghold, and what is particularly interesting is that there are still the fundamentalist Mormons who practice polygamy, a once-common practice in their history. Now, being in Mormon country means you have to be very careful with weed and alcohol; those bastards will spy on you with night goggles when you're in camp and deliver a thousand-dollar fine, plus probation, simply for hitting the peace pipe, which we often did in those days while celebrating a climb over a campfire and rice and beans.

On one rest day, a rainy day, we wandered over near Colorado City. I was reading Jon Krakauer's *Under The Banner of Heaven*, which chronicles the sad, deep sins of the Mormons and their ties to polygamy and the abuse of women, and I was disturbed but curious. We drove through Colorado City, and it was like a pool of incest, a haunting reminder of how the Mormon religion started. People looked inbred and sad; I couldn't bear to look them in their eyes, and we got out of there as quickly as possible.

After several days of wandering the region and trying to stay out of trouble, the weather cleared, and we went back up on Touchstone.

At this point, I was charged and ready to go and wanted nothing else in the world than to be up high in the vertical world. Tim rolled in at two in the morning and pulled into our campsite from Monticello, Utah, where he was living at the time. I demanded we get up as early as possible and everyone obliged. I was surely impatient and too eager. Tim slept slumped over in the front seat of his truck and looked haggard in the morning. Dave and I had already packed everything up the night before.

I was upset at how long we took in the morning and just wanted to charge the climb. We had to wait for the shuttle bus to get a ride in because Zion is closed to cars in the busy season. The tourists looked at us like we were out of our minds, draped in climbing gear. We tried to pay them no mind as we discussed our techniques. We were hoping to do the climb in one push, no bivouac, just up and down in the daylight; we'd be popping beers by nightfall, we hoped.

My selective ADD mind recalls the fourth pitch, a perfect 5.11 splitter that I tried to free climb. At the time, it was at my limit, and, with a few hundred feet of air below my shoes, the effort was thrilling and intoxicating, which is probably why I still remember it. Heart pounding, muscles shaking, I made delicate moves up the face, and barely pulled it off without falling. I was proud of my efforts, and I arrived at the belay awash in adrenaline and psych.

A truly experienced climber will take stock of the situation and decide if there's enough time to complete the climb. I didn't do that; I was just in love and in a trance with the experience. I mean, I didn't analytically think about how we were going to get off this wall or if we had enough time to complete the climb. I just thought, "Holy fuck, this is awesome; this is the life, pushing myself to the limit, ending up higher and higher on a huge sandstone wall, surrounded by bigger sandstone walls. I just want do this forever and never grow old."

I was not yet an experienced climber. I had enough experience on how to climb but not how to climb with style. At this point, Tim's fatigue started showing itself. The guy had only slept a couple hours after driving all night. Dave was calm and collected like always and took the lead, pushing us higher. But the sun was setting as I took the next lead and climbed into the darkness.

We missed a key part of the beta on how to properly climb the Touchstone Wall—you're supposed to rappel down once the steep climbing is over. The route continues, but it wanders up several unimpressive slab pitches, leading to a point of no return.

I'd climbed into the darkness, the night, and we looked at our topo, and we still had about five pitches to go until the summit. Once Tim and Dave came up, we realized that, very unfortunately, Tim did not have a headlamp. He got mad at himself for the forgetfulness, but that's the breaks—sleeplessness leads to forgetting things. And, climbers are almost proud of our ability to improvise.

Then I was getting mad. I started leading up the slab, thinking we're close to having the day over, and I couldn't complete a move. I climbed up and down, and then started yelling, started screaming, like some ancient rage decided to leave my body that day. Dave and Tim sent up the protocol of encouragement, the things climbers always say like "you got it; come on, man, you can do this." I was mad because hours earlier I had been performing at a much higher level, in much steeper more difficult terrain, but the darkness and the fatigue were getting to me, and, in fact, had broken me down until I was a person screaming at a rock face, like yelling at the wind, desperation and frustration getting the best of me. Far from the Zen focus I had just a few hours earlier.

I expelled that energy out of me and got it back together, and hours later we reached the top of the Touchstone Wall. It was one of the most pure moments of fear, bewilderment, and awareness that I've ever had. The moon shined brightly on the surrounding walls, and it was all out of this world but within this world. The world was this wild, astounding, inspiring place. It really was. It was like being on another planet, or in the middle of this deep dream you wondered how you were ever going to be able to get out of or wake up from.

Our escape was a massive gully system that ran alongside the wall. We'd have to rappel down it in order to get back to the base of the climb, so we could get back to the car. But, how would we do that? The shuttles had stopped running long ago and we were miles from our truck. We were out there, that was for sure.

Dave and I had to go first and last on the rappels, so we could shine some light on Tim, who had no light. After a couple rappels, Tim also realized he'd left his climbing shoes on the summit. This was no time to lament; we just had to move. Tim did end up saving the day with cheese and sausage that he'd brought along, and we devoured that like starving men, hungry, so hungry. We'd made seventeen rappels that had taken us several hours. *Was morning approaching, or would the night last forever?* we wondered. None of us had watches, or even a cell phone, so we had no idea what time it was. We reached a point where we could no longer tell where the next rappel was. We couldn't tell and didn't want to be more dangerous than we'd already been, so we just stayed put. We finally accepted the benightment. We sat there cold, fatigued, and frustrated. Dave made a final effort to find the rappel station and scrambled up twenty feet above where Tim and I just sat with our heads in our hands, trying in vain to sleep. He found nothing and sat up there, with his own thoughts of frustration, waiting for the sun to rise.

And it did, like it always does, and it showed us the way. We were a mere two hundred feet about the ground. We rappelled down to the ground and a euphoria struck us that would last for the rest of the day. The light, the surroundings, everything just became magical. The deliriousness of the night turned into a wonderment of light and excitement to just simply exist. We were hungry and we knew there would be food somewhere. And, we'd survived a situation that could have easily gone badly, really badly.

We caught the shuttle and headed straight to the nearby town where we found a buffet. It was just your normal American buffet, nothing fancy or special, but, damn, it felt special. We ate so much food that there's no way they made a dime on us that day. We went back for fourths and fifths and talked to the waitress to ask if we could speak to the manager to tell them just how great the food was. We were high on life, man. We were so high on just climbing and suffering and surviving. It was one of the greatest days of my life.

This is how the addiction to a dirtbag life begins—have a big adventure, get scared and humbled, come back down to the horizontal world and everything seems anew. Normal everyday things become sacred, and then you just want to go up and do it all over again.

So after resting and eating everything we saw for a day and a half, Dave and I went back up. This time we packed a portaledge and a big haul bag, and we went after another so-called moderate aid route, Moonlight Buttress.

It seems silly now to carry so much on a route that barely checks in at a thousand feet long, but we needed to learn. And when my mind drifts back to this climb, it's impossible not to think of it as a work of art from nature/God. A few approach pitches lead up to a laser splitter finger crack that starts and never seems like it's going to finish. The splitter goes for several pitches, like a highway to heaven.

We had plenty of cursing and struggle to get up to that splitter, hauling everything but the kitchen sink. Our first night, we struggled like hell to get that portaledge set up, manual labor at its finest, fighting to put the metal rods together that form the base and let it sit horizontally along the wall, so we could have a small place to sleep for the night. It felt so awkward, and I went to anger much quicker than Dave, cursing at the damn thing. Finally, and patiently, Dave got it set up, and we had our dinner of one shared beer and some sort of food that we ate out of a can with the nut tool, the same tool we shoved into cracks to get the cams and nuts out, so the tool was covered in aluminum, grime, and dirt.

Like a good completed day of manual labor, we felt hard-earned satisfaction, relieved to have our perch on this sandstone wall in a canyon of sandstone walls, with trees below looking like small bushes, and birds circling and swerving below you and among you. There's something to be said for living a life among the birds.

The struggle continued into the next day, taking down the portaledge, packing, and moving upward. The progress was simple, and the cracks were perfect, even better for free climbing, but we were not there yet. We were just a couple of hard-working guys, learning the mechanics of aid climbing, paying our dues for bigger climbs ahead.

The struggle was relieved at the top. We were awash with relief and success. We shook hands and proudly took stock of a hard-earned view as the sun went down. A week without showering, two walls, and a lot of wandering around the weird western Utah, it was time to go on to whatever would be next.

On the trail down, it was dark, and we slowly moved down with our ropes and large haul bag, happy as pigs in shit. A party of three passed us, with a couple women. They smelled clean and wonderful, like a flower in spring, showing us everything that was right in the world, and they probably held their noses as we passed. That night, we packed up the truck and drove back to Indian Creek.

Chapter 25

Once the desert got too hot, I returned back to the mountains, much as the Utes would do back in the day. I was in some sort of carnal survival mode; I knew I loved climbing, and I just thought I should do what I needed to do to continue climbing.

There was always a welcoming feeling to being back in Gunnison; after all, it was all the home I really had—I was home when I was in Illinois, but, in Gunny, I felt at home, among my people. I returned to my dishwashing gig in Crested Butte and moved into an apartment in Gunny with my friend Phil.

The apartment complex soon became an elaborate basecamp for our friends, with two of us living there and paying rent, but there was always someone camping out in their RV in the parking lot or someone crashed out on the couch. Our good friends Amber and Sara lived next door, and the Cebolla Lodge, as it was called, became a commune of sorts.

Looking back, I wonder why I didn't have more drive, more motivation. I would put myself through great pains to climb a big wall, but I didn't have any desire to start a career. My writing was sporadic, a path I was on but not fully dedicated to. I had an ocean of time to sit upon, and all I did was float.

My dishwashing gig took up much of my time. I considered myself a master of the trade. I would even let the dishes pile sky high just to see how quickly I could make the pile dissipate. I would save money by hitchhiking up to Crested Butte from Gunnison instead of driving. All sorts of characters would pick me up, but some nights I'd sit at the hitchhiking post for an hour, desperate for a ride, wondering to myself why I would be so cheap as to not drive.

I guess in many ways this was the end of the era of being by yourself: cell phones were still archaic, no social media, just you and your thoughts. Once I got into a rhythm, I started writing again. All the stories I wrote were in the style of what the *Mountain Gazette* would publish. My writing mentor in college, George Sibley, was a longtime contributor, and the editor of the *Gazette,* John Fayhee, adored Sibley and his work, so he would listen to him when he recommended a piece. The *Mountain Gazette* was a free, monthly publication, and I even decided to become the delivery boy, for some extra cash once a month, hoping that would build some street cred with Fayhee.

The *Gazette* had a history that went back to Edward Abbey and Hunter S. Thompson, and all the stories were full of adventure and rebels and the American West that I'd been obsessed with since I started reading Kerouac. I wanted to join the lineage. I regularly submitted stories to Fayhee, and, after a couple highly edited successes, he just started saying no. I took it personally, of course— what writer doesn't take things personally? Then, after some prying as to why he wasn't accepting my submissions, he delivered the hard blow that was the truth: I needed to learn the craft. I had the prose and poetry but, embarrassingly, lacked some of the basics needed to publish. He noted that every piece of mine had to have an edit every sentence. I was trying to break the rules before I learned them. His final line in the message: You need to get a basic writing job to learn the craft.

I wasn't ready to get a steady job, to sit at a desk and be patient and learn a craft with an editor by my side, coaching me on the art of writing. I just wanted to be stoned and wash dishes, and travel and climb rocks, and live with my head in the clouds. Some say the brain doesn't stop growing until the midtwenties; I was a little past that, but maybe my brain was on a late growth spurt. Maybe I just lacked discipline. So I continued to write with bad grammar and punctuation, scribbling out my dreams at the coffeeshop, handwritten dreams and words that have since disappeared, but, thankfully, the dream did not disappear.

Life continued to give me art and inspiration. I became acquainted with a woman named Corrina, who was a yoga teacher and had the looks of a goddess. She told me that her parents named her after the Bob Dylan song, "Corrina, Corrina." They must have known she was going to be a heartbreaker:

Corrina, Corrina,

Gal you're on my mind

Corrina, Corrina,

I'm a thinkin' 'bout you baby

I just can't keep from crying

Like the rules of writing, I lacked any sense in the unwritten rules of love—I just dove in headfirst with true emotion and never paced myself or took a cautious approach. Like the song told me, I knew Corrina would hurt me.

She brought me into her bedroom, and, after that, I was under her trance. Whenever we would be apart, I would long for her, and, whenever we were together, I just wanted to love her. I came on too strong and scared her off. When she ultimately broke up with me, the pains of many years before all came back. I was still holding on to that pain from Cherise, so many years before, so long ago then that it felt like a lifetime ago, but the heart remembers so deeply.

The cycles of Gunnison Valley living happened like they always do: the reluctant and eventually blissful, fleeting summer, the nostalgic fall leading into the winter. I moved out of my apartment in Gunnison and couch surfed much of the fall. When winter approached, I sold my truck and bought a cheaper car; I would use all the money for my winter travels. I didn't know where I would end up, I just knew I would start in Mexico again and see where that led me.

Chapter 26

All this time I was finding myself

And I didn't know I was lost

—Aloe Blacc, "Wake Me Up"

I rolled out for my third Mexico trip with Two Tent. He'd been living out in Oregon for the last few years, and it was nice to finally have him back in Colorado. We would be picking up Mark in San Antonio and then meeting Scott there. I had everything I owned in a little 1988 Mazda compact car.

A great ice storm enveloped Texas that fateful January day, and all the years of training with winter driving in Colorado surely helped us stay on the road. Nothing could protect us from other drivers; we probably saw forty cars and semitrucks that had driven off the road. At times, the ice would just catch your car, and you would be swerving out of control, your rear end giving out. We managed to stay on the road, but the driving was much slower than we'd anticipated, and we stopped off in small Texas highway town to try to find a place to rest our weary bones.

The town was incredibly sketchy, overrun by characters of the night. Two Tent had never even paid to stay in a hotel before, and he insisted that we keep looking for cheaper prices, and the motels got worse and worse as we went through this process. Dirtbag instincts can be good; they can save you money; sometimes, they can guide you in the wrong direction, and they led us to a drug den of a motel, at the end of the line of sketchy motels. But, we just needed a place to sleep for a few hours, right?

Ten minutes in, we had a pimp knocking on our door. We didn't answer but looked out the peephole to his sketchy face. Then the phone rang, and it's a guy looking for sex. After that, we proceeded to put the dresser up against the door of the motel. We slept restlessly and got back on the highway to pick up Mark and cross over into Mexico.

Mark was easy to pick out at the airport: he stands six-foot-two with wild, goofy blond hair and blue eyes—he stood out even more in Mexico. Mark had one week, as did Two Tent; they were seeking reprieve from the cold, Crested Butte winter. Scott and I had been raving about Potrero since our perfect month there the year before.

The storm was socked in. Instead of bluebird skies and perfect temperatures, the sky was graybird, and a fog permeated the canyon. It had a Gothic vibe to it, and, instead of an electric feeling of stoke like the year before, the place seemed lethargic and damp. We all made the best of it. Two Tent and Mark didn't know any difference in the place anyway, but Scott and I knew just how good it could be. After a few days of cragging, we needed a rest day, and the sky was blue for the first time on the trip. The next day, it was back to gray skies. Two Tent and Mark had left, and Scott and I decided to hit the road.

This was my second winter of just floating, but this winter I had even less of a plan than before. I thought I'd maybe just stay in Mexico all winter, but Scott needed a ride to Prescott, Arizona, where he was in graduate school, so I volunteered to give him a lift. I just made him promise we could visit Joshua Tree, California, which was on the list of places I could end up, just for the winter.

We drove and drove across the bottom of the country. We were pulled over three times in the middle of the night along the border. My car was bursting at the seams with everything I owned, plus Scott's gear. At one point, they asked if they could search the car; I said, no, I know my rights, and you have no probable cause. They let us go. We drove through the night into the next day. We tried to climb at Cochise in Arizona but got snowed out. We kept driving and driving, hoping to drive away from the weather. Finally, we headed to California to Joshua Tree, arriving in the middle of the night.

Was Joshua Tree the place I needed to be? It had a history of being the climbers' winter hangout in Southern California. The weather was supposed to be perfect for climbing in the winter, and a winter without snow appealed to me very much. I knew I needed to get a job; I didn't save enough money to not work all winter, even for the meager funds I'd need just to eat and climb all day.

Over the next couple days, Joshua Tree won me over. The blue skies finally revealed themselves, and we basked in the sun and scared ourselves on the granite slabs and domes. The J-Trees, thousands of them, unique and stretching out, like they were doing yoga, extended across the landscape for miles and miles; there was no end in sight to the landscape, just like the sky above. There were plenty of other climbers around, and I knew I could count on them for partners. After a short two-day trial, I decided I wanted to stay. I just needed a part-time job.

I knew my work ethic could get me a gig if I could just get my foot in the door somewhere. In my mind, there was only one place, Crossroads, the restaurant that served the needs of climbers from coffee to lunch to beers to dinners. It was where everyone went, and I saw my in. I walked in the place and told them I was the greatest dishwasher this side of the Mississippi. The owner kinda looked at me as to say, "So what?" But like almost always, they needed a dishwasher, because the dishwasher is the most transient and temporary of all jobs, and, three days later, after taking Scott back to Arizona, I was working my first shift.

Alone in Southern California. I could practically hear the Eagles' music in the landscape—that land where it's always sunny, where America is on the edge, nowhere else to expand our empire, so it blossoms into this land of fast cars and tank tops and bikinis. Joshua Tree stands as an oasis among the madness, the one place humans let stand alone. I knew it was where I could make my stand, to climb a winter.

Of course, I lived in a tent in Hidden Valley, the main climbers' campground. I used a pay phone for calls. I didn't have a computer, and the only way people could get ahold of me was by calling Crossroads, which did happen, and I'd be at the dishwashing sink, still washing away among the soap and the grime, catching up with my friends who seemed very much stoked for me that I'd committed to a winter of dirtbagging in J-Tree.

One of those guys was my buddy Adam, who seemed more stoked for me than I was stoked for me. We went to college together, and he was like many of my adventurous friends from college, wild and hungry for all types of experiences. Though he didn't know it, he was convincing me of how awesome my life was. In my own mind, I was lost and searching for something I'd yet to identify. I just knew I had to be uncomfortable and on the edge. Joshua Tree was certainly the edge.

On the edge of America, there are always the freaks. In climbing, everyone used to be a freak, but now it's more mainstream; the pockets still exist though, and, at the time, it was only five bucks a night to camp in Joshua Tree, and, if you were creative enough, you could stay well past the fourteen-day limit. I needed to stay past that limit; I didn't have any money for rent or any desire to live indoors. I just wanted to be wild and free among the rocks and to call them my rightful home.

My tent, my home, had poetry scribbled on the walls. I kept a daily journal of every dime that I spent; after all, I was living on washing dishes three days a week. There were leftovers though, and I ate as much as I ever needed. My stomach was fed, and it left only my spirit to be fed.

The landscape fed my spirit but also left me hungry, a kind of hunger I couldn't understand at the time. It also provided me with a home. There were others too, the freaks from the full-time climbing tribe of which I would be included in and then the weekend climbers who would come and go from the city.

Of course, the first challenge was to solicit partners, finding someone I could trust and, equally as important, whose company I could enjoy. Right away, I noticed the dirtbag-hippie stronghold, which operated out of Camp 17. There were many, many of them, and their camp carried an aura from the past of California climbing. They were all hippies, but everyone, of course, carried the torch of dirtbag climbing in their own way. Some wore bandanas and had elaborate free solo circuits in the domes surrounding camp. They seemed to live free. There were ten guys for every girl in the hardcore day-to-day crowd, which made me think I'd have a very lonely winter in the female front.

But I was there to climb, and I was there to figure myself out, even if I did not realize that at the time. It was an ecstatic relief to be wearing a tank top in the winter, my skin tanned and blessed from getting touched by the Southern California sun. I felt like I'd gotten away with something, like I'd escaped the cold and found my haven for the winter.

I found one of my first climbing partners in one of the few women I'd met around, a cook where I worked. She was a beautiful Asian woman who'd graduated from Yale and had a yearning to just be a climber in California. Damn, did I respect that. She had a boyfriend, but she was still looking for climbing partners, so we teamed up every now and again. At work, we initially developed the camaraderie between cook and dishwasher that is often hard to obtain. My street cred as a climber gave me a fast track to being accepted at the restaurant.

Two other cooks, local boys from the town of Joshua Tree, which was the smallest town I'd ever lived in, were stoner dudes who were curious about climbing. One had just spent time in prison and had used hard drugs, but he was now clean from all that and had a glimmer of hope. Another was younger and had that look in his eye that maybe he wanted something different in life than just the day-to-day motions of eat, work, sleep, repeat.

The head cook was the co-owner, who owned the joint with her mother. Now, I've seen and heard some shit in the back of kitchens—you want to talk about a place with a lack of filter for language, it's a kitchen hidden away from the customers—but I'd never heard a mouth like the one the daughter had. She cussed and yelled so frequently that I think everyone, including myself, was scared of her in a certain sort of way. But, no matter how deep and profane her language was, she never talked to me directly in that way, and we maintained sweet relations.

So just like that, in a couple weeks, I had a community of sorts, at least a few people who knew my name and would recognize me. That was a huge relief because I think I had a deep fear of being swallowed by the vast loneliness of modern life, being in a new, strange place, all alone, without a clue where I was going in my life. But sometimes, it's not about where you're going, it's about where you are.

Too Strong Dave was another character that came into my life, and how couldn't he?—he was the local guy, always posted up at the bar at the café. His arms were like cannons; apparently he was an arm wrestling champion. He was intimidating, but he was a climber, and, usually, great climbers are also great men.

After two weeks of recognizing that I wasn't just there for a short time, he opened up and started asking me about what I'd climbed that day. When I would tell him, like say the time I was working on Spiderline, an 11c that looks like a 5.9, he would have some spot-on comment about the delicate nature of the line, or exactly how difficult the crux was. He was a walking, talking guidebook, and, by identifying that I was a new guy on the scene, which was humbling going through the grades and the classic climbs, he was a part of my quest to experience Joshua Tree.

My lineup of climbing partners was very much lacking, and I solicited people from camp, as often happens in places like J-Tree. It was like the danger of taking a girl you didn't know home from the bar. One guy I climbed with told me he'd finally recovered from a broken leg he'd obtained in a climbing fall. He promptly smoked a bowl and then tried to lead Tax Man, a tricky 10a, and shaked his way up it, scaring the shit out of me. His erratic movement and lack of confidence was a buzzkill, and I found a way to act like I had something else to do for the rest of the day.

One of my regular climbing partners was a bitter British guy, who was always uttering and mumbling negative statements about everything. He was like a friend by default, by association, because we had ended up camping next to one another, and we were both climbers looking for someone to climb with. I liked him; deep down he was a good guy, but my sensitive and delicate nature could not handle such negativity. He even would complain about how short and stupid the climbs were in J-Tree, which is a commonly uttered statement; not everyone finds the same beauty in the same things, but, when he left camp, I vowed to only surround myself with positive people.

And as the weeks passed and I passed my fourteen-day limit, I stayed anyways. I would have requested a late checkout, but there was no one to call. I wrote these words in a sharpie on my sleeping pad:

I am somewhere between a fourteen-day camping limit

And living the dream

Positivity was part of the equation; it is perhaps one of the most important ingredients to a healthy climbing life. But, I was lonely, and I knew it. I wanted the comfort of a woman, but there were very few around, and I still lacked having much game. Sure, I'd attracted women in Gunny, but those were women who knew me and my backstory—I was someone there, but I was no one in J-Tree, just a dude who had no money and washed dishes and climbed rocks.

And therein laid my problem. I didn't have intention or specific goals. I was just there, floating. Now I know the truth: Life is a river you're going down, quickly and swiftly, like a spring runoff. If you can take a second and scope that river out to see where you're going and where the obstacles are, you'll be better off. Life is like that river, and, though there are so many unpredictable aspects of life, the shape that a life takes and the stages of that life are predictable.

I knew I was blessed with the opportunity to live a good life in America. Perhaps I knew it too much, because I was willing to live with such little money it astounded everyone back home in Illinois. I figured money would always be there, and I could simply work and earn it if I really ever needed to, and that is a blessing, a confidence that the man who has never had money could never have.

The *why I was there* I could have never understood at the time. *I wanted to climb* would have been my answer. The weekend warriors who frequented J-Tree would always be jealous of me when I told them how long I was staying for. That would immediately make them think of work on Monday, and they would think of me climbing on Monday. I would carry that aura of living the dream in our conversation, but it was an illusion. There was just so much that was missing. If it really came down to it, I was as jealous of those people as they were of me. Jealous of their significant others, their stability, their jobs, well, maybe not their jobs, but I was jealous that they had a life plan set into action.

And therein lived my battle, my struggle. I was out in Joshua Tree because, after eighteen years of schooling, I still didn't know what to do for a career. I didn't want to fight, I didn't want to teach, I didn't want to research, and I didn't want to study in classrooms anymore. I felt like I was given a world of opportunity, and I still passed on every opportunity except that opportunity to climb rocks and live outside.

And even that was illegal. People could rape and pillage nature and build second-home mansions on top of rocks legally, but for little old me to live in a tent on public lands among the rocks was illegal. It gave me a challenge though, living in my tent there. I studied the rangers and their habits, and they were predictable. They did their rounds at the same time every morning, so all I had to do was move my car to the day-use area and they wouldn't recognize it or record my license plate number to notice the number of days I was in the campground. It was fun, and when other people got busted for overstaying and had to leave, I was proud of my ways. I would climb up on the rocks behind camp when the rangers did their patrol and watch them, like the rocks protected me and the place I'd chosen to call home for the season.

Some of the folks who had been kicked out still returned, like this girl they called The Mayor, a hippie girl who barely climbed but was part of the scene, and she was a girl, so she was more than appreciated by the community. She had dreads and rarely showered, and she oozed California hippie. Then, I was slowly starting to become more civilized, showering more and keeping my hair cut to a buzz, and I was less and less into the hippie culture of how I dressed and presented my looks. But, the hippie culture should, and I hope always will, be ingrained into American culture. Because, with intentions, hippies represent everything good about America, and they balance out our war cries and our industrial nature that's out to conquer the world. The hippie says conquer yourself and nothing else. And so does the dirtbag, in her or his or her own way. The Mayor returned, again and again, and got kicked out, again and again. She was a rebel, even if her only cause was to live a peaceful, simple life in J-Tree. I'd say that's a rebel with a righteous cause.

To live this life, there were customs and practices that had been developed over time, since the first hippies descended upon J-Tree in numbers large enough to make them a force to be reckoned with. I knew the story, the history; we all did. California's climbing history is better documented than any other aspect of American climbing. One of those rituals in J-Tree was to free solo.

J-Tree has its funk, its uniqueness that is so strong it repels the climber not able to appreciate its flavor, but it leaves another sort of climber so entranced with the lifestyle that he or she falls in love with it. I was certainly of the latter; as lost as I was, I was in love.

I'd done some free solo climbing before J-Tree, but they were angsty endeavors. I would be fed up with school and tired of studying and sitting and didn't have a partner, so I'd head out to Taylor Canyon and climb up some 5.6s and 5.7s until my mind calmed down. They were moderate climbs, but, if I would have fallen, I would have died, and one day I was forced to down climb a hundred feet of 5.6 and pretty much scared the shit out of myself enough to realize that free soloing wasn't for me. My ADD mind could create a hyper focus in most dangerous climbing situations, but free solo climbing was not one of them. At least not for two hundred or more feet. Perhaps it was just my inner voice saying, "This is stupid—get back to the ground and get a rope."

In J-Tree it's different. There are some just downright fantastic 5.4s, 5.5s, and 5.6s that can be soloed. They have hand jams so good they basically swallow your body, and it would be nearly impossible to fall off of them. Plus, many are a minute from camp. They practically beg you to climb them. And so I would, and so would many of the climbers from camp. It became a ritual of sorts. Climb on ropes all day, then finish up with a solo to the top of some dome, watch the sunset, drink a beer, take a puff, and then scurry back down.

These were the leisure solos, and then there were the hardcores. It all began in the era of my literary hero, John Long in the 1970s. Like Two Strong Dave, Long didn't have the typical super lean build that most strong climbers had; he had the looks of a bodybuilder. Long could (can) write like a bird flies, the wind blows, and a climber climbs. His stories of the original hard free solos in J-Tree are legends; he started it off but quickly passed the torch to John Bachar, an original Stonemaster, who took free soloing to a higher level than anyone down in Southern California. The images of Bachar climbing stunning lines in J-Tree that many of us could barely do with a rope make the mind spin, like, what, how could he?

The John Bachar of my time in J-Tree was Michael Reardon. Reardon had the look of an 80s hair band rocker—which he actually was—with wild golden-blond hair and deep blue eyes that were like looking into a clear mountain lake. Reardon was not only around, he was everywhere. He soloed everything Bachar could and then ushered in a new level, with Equinox, a 5.13 finger crack, and many other standard-setting climbs. He loved Bachar and even made a movie about him; they grew into a friendship of mutual admiration and respect.

I was getting more comfortable with my soloing, but I could only live in imagination and try to grasp what it felt like to be at the top of the free solo game. To have eighty feet of air below you with only your fingertips in a crack and your feet pasted delicately on the wall, knowing that's all that's between you and certain death, or worse, must be exhilarating beyond description. Goddamn, that's gotta be like the first high from a serious drug, or like a bird flying—how could we mere mortals understand the joys that climbing gods experience?

I guess these guys were bigger than life. Shortly after my J-Tree season, Bachar died in a free solo accident near Mammoth, California. And shortly after that, Reardon died in Ireland, swept away by a rogue wave after he had soloed some sea cliffs. Maybe they rolled the dice one too many times, or God just had other plans for their energy that could not be contained in a human body.

John Long, too, came crashing down to earth in an accident, in the climbing gym of all places, after he failed to fully tie his bowline knot properly. Luckily he survived, with only a broken leg. While the world will never again see these three in J-Tree confidently soloing steep terrain, engaged in an ecstasy and confidence few ever feel, I know for sure the legends are alive in campfire stories, and a select breed is following in their footsteps.

I had a couple soloing moments that I clearly remember. The first was a 5.9 handcrack, right in the campground. I'd climbed it a week before, and it had very sharp edges in the crack—J-Tree is famous for its razor-sharp edges— and because I couldn't decide whether I wanted to face the left side of my body in the dihedral or the right side, it seemed awkward. But one day I was climbing on Intersection Rock, and I was just looking over staring at it. I felt calm and in the moment, so, when we were done climbing over there, I stood under it and thought about whether I should solo it.

And I did. I started up, with the feelings of nervousness and freedom intertwined. Once I started climbing, the jams seemed to swallow my hands, and it felt easier than when I had a rack of gear and a rope—nothing to weigh me down, nothing to make it awkward when shifting around in the crack. Forty feet up, when you're entering a zone where life as you know it would be over if you fell, was the best moment; endorphins and adrenaline released, a feeling of strength and peace overcame me. I could see how that would be addicting. I drove into work that evening on the high, blasting Hendrix from the car stereo.

I saw J-Tree from the lens of a climber, the climber who washed dishes, living hand to mouth. When I arrived at the restaurant, a pile of thirty bacon trays from the morning awaited me. Any high I was riding had to face that. Plus, I was a college graduate, and what I was doing for a living, after all that money spent on an education, was one of the most basic jobs out there. Then I'd look around, and most of the clientele were climbers and the cook just across the kitchen was a graduate from Yale, so I felt a little more at peace. And then I'd leave with leftovers that would fuel the fire to climb another day.

The clientele, the people, they had everything I needed, and I've felt that way for some time now, that all I need is a simple life of climbing and good people. And there are lot of good people, but our lives are made up of our people, those who speak the same language, and not just the English language, or even the talk of climbers, but the language of the heart, and what the heart wants, and what you want out of life.

Whenever I was washing dishes, I would always look out and scan the crowd and go out and talk if I knew someone. Sometimes I'd just see a table, and I could tell they were talking about a specific climb because someone would start acting out the moves, miming them, with hands in the air, even a knee raised to accentuate the foot movement, facial expression awash in the magic that is climbing.

There was as much weirdness as there was magic. The crew then, the hippies, liked to throw naked parties. Seemed very California. They invited me to one in town, and I went over there fully clothed. There was like one naked chick and fifteen dudes. I didn't stay long.

A couple weeks later, they'd arranged another naked party, a disco dance party on top of The Blob, a formation right there in camp that had some super fun, easy hand cracks leading to the top. It was a ritual to climb up there, to watch the sunset, or just take a quick lap while people were lounging in the heat of the day.

Chapter 27

I found out about the naked disco dance party by social media, the original social media, The Mayor and some hippie dudes were walking around camp yelling: "Disco Dance Party on The Blob tonight...BYOB."

Then The Mayor said, "And it's a *naked* disco dance party!"

And one of the guys said, "Don't advertise that! You'll just attract more dudes!"

I knew there would be lots of dudes, judging by the nature of the culture, there and then, so the party was hardly intriguing. Plus, the next day I had plans to get a lot of climbing in, and I knew that would never happen if I partied into the night.

I did find the crew interesting though. I don't know if they knew I was a writer, shit, I didn't really even know if I was really a writer then, but I knew they were muses in many ways. They were dirtbag rebels for sure. They messed with tourists, were loud at night, and free soloed in costumes. They were everything climbers were in the J-Tree golden age of the seventies.

One of their antics I found amusing was RV surfing. An RV would inevitably roll through camp, trying to find a site, and almost always the sites were full of dirtbag climbers, so they had to continue elsewhere to find a site. Their huge RVs seemed out of place in the little dirtbag climber camp haven, and all of the comforts that go along with that lifestyle. The drivers, perched high above, gazed out into camp to see all these dirtbag climbers and probably realized this was not the camp for them. And, just when that would happen, someone would decide to RV surf. They climbed up the ladder on the back (bonus points if they were naked, of course) and stood proudly on the top of the RV, basking in cheers from their watching friends.

My camp was just down the way from theirs, so I'd catch the cheers first, and then look up to see ass cheeks, and a naked dude, in broad daylight, standing atop some RV with a name like *The Explorer*, and I had to laugh. They were raw, silly, and ambitious without much direction. I liked them.

I still didn't want to go to the disco party. I wanted to sleep. When the time came around for sleep, I'd already had a nightcap, brushed my teeth, said my prayers and was reading to fall asleep, but the party got louder and louder, and I had no choice but to follow the statement, "If you can't beat 'em, join 'em."

I stumbled out of my tent and thought about how many beers I had in my cooler, followed by, *What should I wear?* Wait, it's a naked party. I don't have to worry about that, and I stumbled more, to the glowing lights atop The Blob.

As I moved around in the bushes at the base of The Blob, I heard other rustling. There were two other people, a guy from Switzerland, and another guy with a backpack full of beer, who looked quite clueless as to how he was going to get to the party. He offered me some beers if I would help get him up there.

I shined my headlamp on the wall, and we traversed around to an easy hand crack. I started up, the jams so good they swallowed my hand, and it was like an anchor, ensuring that I wouldn't fall fifty feet below into the talus. Backpack Full of Beer Guy is behind me, and he starts to make some odd noises. I mean, this crack was as easy as they come. I yelled down to make sure everything was okay.

"Yeah, I'm fine," he assured me. "But the problem is I've never actually climbed before."

Holy fuck, I thought to myself. I can't be responsible for this; I have to talk him out of it. So I gently and quietly told him he should probably retreat. He did and, thankfully, didn't crash down to the earth, ending his life and surely ending the party. I climbed up, the ground not visible because of the dark; the top was lit up with hues of neon green, red, and blue that were permeating from the summit.

Naked hippies atop a rock with disco music and the stars for a ceiling. My primal instincts scanned the crowd: three women, not bad, better than one. A big dreadlocked man looked at me and said,

"Welcome." The Mayor was up there, twirling these balls that changed colors from red to green to purple. It actually felt a little magical up there. She quietly suggested that I get naked, so I did.

The sensation was somewhere between liberation and curiosity. I wouldn't have been up there if they hadn't kept me awake, but, now that I was there, it's a sight to behold. The underground culture of J-Tree in their element. We danced to disco music, uninhibited; bottles and joints were passed.

This was just the beginning. After the enjoyment of dancing naked on the top of a granite dome passed, a suggestion was made: "Let's do the chasm."

I'd heard about this "chasm," a long series of chimneys and tunnels usually saved for debaucherous situations like this one. Headlamps were considered cheating. Sobriety too. So a dozen or so of us retreated from The Blob, everyone headed in different directions. We all ended up at a two biker dudes' campsite. One was recovering from a crash. They liked the craziness in attendance, if nothing else, to accompany their whiskey drinking. One guy was now wearing a bunny suit. Some fire torches came out of nowhere.

Soon, the guy in the bunny suit was leading ten naked people and me through camp. I was clothed because I didn't want to get arrested for public indecency in a national park. I was willing to take calculated risks for breaking rules, but this was way out of my comfort zone.

Someone questioned why I had my clothes on. "This event needs to be recorded," I claimed, thinking that if a ranger shows up, I'll be happy to have something on.

"Well, if there's one thing we learned from Hunter S. Thompson, it was to participate," he answered.

Naked again, I entered a chimney, burrowing into a granite cliff, away from the moonlight into pure darkness. "The chasm of doooom," someone yelled, words echoing into the cave.

Move by move, beta was shared through the chimney, climbers

tunneling, squeezing and down climbing; we passed half an hour with no headlamps, only the shared word from above in the long tunnel up and then down through the granite rock. I wondered, *Where are we going?*

Then we emerged at a ledge, exposed and interwoven in a granite world, one where the stars were comforting. A tribe of tattooed, naked climbers, smoke poured from mouths, and cold air blew on our skin. We looked out onto the endless granite and Joshua trees, each their own shape, with every limb going its own direction, barely visible by the moonlight.

Down climbing the chasm was horrible, scraping skin, claustrophobic thoughts in the dark world. My mood lightened for a second when someone said, "Watch your package here."

Just when I'd had enough, there's an opening: the sand, the boulders, the cactuses the horizontal world. We ran on the road again, back to camp, no cars, only the pat of bare feet on pavement, inhalations and exhalations. The bunny led, fire torches behind him. If the law were to drive by, it could be bad.

We arrived in camp. The crew, through inspiration or annoyance, invited me into their group. I looked up to The Blob; granite clearly lit up by the moon is stunning. Camp was completely quiet. My tent, weathered badly by the wind, poles sticking through the nylon, begged me to enter, to another dream.

There were more weeks of desert dreaming, and then I was completely burnt out. Worn ragged by the wind, granite, and tent living, I knew there was only one place I wanted to be: the Gunnison Valley.

With the swaying Joshua trees in my rearview mirror, I headed back home to Colorado. Still ragged, I only had a couple weeks before another double marathon of driving. I had a wedding for my dear friends in Austin, Texas, and then I would drive home to see my parents. Whenever I'd be on the road, I would rarely meet single women, so that was exactly what was on my mind when I returned to Gunny. And, just before driving down south to Texas, I met one, a sweet redhead college student, shy as could be but possessing the attraction that no logic could explain.

So I did my epic drive, down to the south of Texas where they love everything big, and my friends wed in a wonderful ceremony, and I wondered when I would find my soul mate whom I would marry. Then in Illinois, I visited my family. My Dad was cleaning out my car a bit; it needed it because, after all, I'd been living out of it for months on end. He opened up the trunk and pulled back the layer before the spare tire. He was amazed at what he found, and so was I. A bag of beans from Mexico had slipped back there and so had some dirt from God knows where. Somehow, someway, the beans had sprouted and were growing in the dirt. Yes, my dirtbag mobile that I got for a thousand bucks, was not only a good deal, but she was fertile. And it did just fine across the Midwest, enduring the painful flatness and boredom that is Kansas, and finally, finally, taking my weary bones back home to Gunny.

Chapter 28

The coming home was the sweetest part of the journey back in those days. Perhaps it was my lack of purpose, because, in Gunny, I had more purpose. I had a community that knew me and supported me, and I had a dishwashing gig in Crested Butte I could always go back to. The greening of the landscape excited the poet in me, and so did the promise of being with a woman.

That summer I dirtbagged it even more than the one before, living in a tent in my friend's front yard at the Cebolla Lodge, the same complex I'd lived at the year before. The dirtbags had taken over. There were friends living in campers in the parking lot, and the two apartments next to each other were occupied by my friends. For every person paying rent, there was a dirtbag living for free. We devised systems to pay each other back: washing dishes, cleaning up, a twenty-dollar bill every once in a while. The only person not too happy with the arrangement was the landlord, but he could do little to stop us; we had our dirtbag troops amassed at the line of battle, and he was still getting his money for rent, and everything was being taken care of. Plus the landlord was something of a drunk/drug user, and our liberal interpretation of the lease agreement by whoever was actually paying rent found it acceptable to use the space on our dirtbag terms.

Every decision was still about freedom, but I realized freedom is nothing without love. Yes, freedom is our war cry, that stuff that makes up rock 'n' roll songs, that thing America is all about, but I'd studied freedom and drank freedom and lived on freedom, and it was simply not enough.

Megan was the shyest girl I'd ever dated. She was a cute little redhead, a college student, and it took me forever to get her to open up and share about herself. We had little recreational activities in common, so we made one up: fishing. I like fishing, but there are always ten other things I'd rather do. So we bought a fishing pole together, and we used it as our excuse to do something.

The first night we spent together, she invited me up into her room—she had to, since I was living in my friend's front yard in a tent, so I had no place to invite her to. As we lay under the covers, she put on some music, Citizen Cope. It was the same record that Corrina and I had listened to when we were together, and it was like love had been on pause for a year. I couldn't believe she put on that music, and, of course, I didn't say anything, and I'd never told anyone because how can you explain the magic of things like that. I suppose that is why I write, so I can tell you.

Goddamn it had been a long, lonely year. Like my man Willie Nelson sang though:

One night of love can't make up for six nights alone

But I'd rather have one than none Lord cause I'm flesh and bone

Fishing adventures led to hiking, and one weekend before she was set to leave after the summer—why do they always leave the mountains after the summer?—we planned a final excursion. We packed up our backpacks and a tent, put the fishing pole on just in case and hiked toward an alpine lake. It was called Blue Lake, and I'm sure every mountain town has a Blue Lake or a Green Lake, or two of both, Crested Butte does, and we spent the good part of the day hiking toward it, and we assembled home in the form of a tent, and, just then, when camp was assembled, a massive lightning storm broke out.

We just waited it out in the tent. The intensity of nature and lightning erupted into the tent, and we came alive, making love all night. It was as if we were the only two people on the planet, intertwined as one. In the morning we hiked out, and a couple weeks later she left town.

I left town after the fall, when winter rolled around. I was suffering from tendonitis and had been resting from climbing. Without climbing, I felt aimless. I started writing more, but, for the athlete, mere mental exercise will not suffice. I was looking for an excuse to hit the road; I had to, and, when my friend Sara, whose lawn I'd been living in all season, needed help moving to Salt Lake City, Utah, I offered my assistance.

Sara was like my little sister; there were no romantic interests there, only a friendship cemented in a way that all my friendships were made: through climbing and sharing the dirtbag lifestyle. She'd been recruited by our friend Adam to work in a youth wilderness therapy-type place in Salt Lake and had taken the job.

Again, like I had the last three winters, I liquidated my possessions, which weren't that many since I was already living out of my car, and blasted off before winter really settled in the Gunnison Valley. I was on my way to Salt Lake City.

In Salt Lake, I helped Sara move into her new place and stayed on her couch a few times. I stayed on Adam's couch a few times too. He was more than generous. He was also happy and had found direction, so I looked to him for answers. He did all the sports—climbing, running, boating, biking—but his true passion was skiing. He'd formed a crew, called the Skier Boyz, which was basically a goofy outlet for twentysomething skiers to be silly and ski. I was jealous of him, but, through his gestures of an open door and an open couch, I deeply appreciated him and his generosity.

After three weeks of couch surfing, partying, and exploring the city, I was already low on money. I didn't have much saved and city living was expensive. I decided I'd have to look for a job. I talked to Sara and her roommate, and they agreed that I could stay in their basement for a couple hundred bucks a month until I figured things out.

I got a job washing dishes, always washing dishes, at a vegan restaurant. Adam thought that was so cool. He was able to have enthusiasm for my life when I had none. He had the stoke, the psych, the fire, whatever you want to call it. I did not. Well, I did, I guess—I was just on a hiatus of being psyched. Depressed. Not seeing light. It didn't help that I was immersed in the smog of the city and rarely left that. My car broke down, and I was too lazy and poor to fix it. I rode my bike everywhere and breathed in that awful brown smog that settles in Salt Lake in the winter. As bad as Los Angeles they say.

My routine consisted of working late-night dishwashing shifts, sleeping in until noon, and then doing the same thing over the next day. I rarely exercised. I felt the darkness deeply. I was living in a concrete basement where I could almost see my breath. The depression was not how it was years before though; it was just like waiting out a storm.

I began to write. Writing became my exercise, and I would go to the library and coffeeshops for hours on end and create stories, prose. There was a deep, yearning and longing, and I channeled that into my notebook. I'd gotten my first laptop as a hand-me-down, and I started pitching stories to magazines, and I actually got some published. And then, after peeking around in the library and finding a section full of zines, I decided to publish my own zine.

The modern zine is a byproduct of skate culture, of which I am not a part of but I can respect it. They were black and white, stapled together, forms of free speech and expression. I loved the canvas but didn't necessarily appreciate the art. Then I discovered the *Dishwasher* zine by Pete Jordan.

Dishwasher Pete was a lazy man, a dirtbag at heart, without the climbing, who made an attempt to wash dishes in all fifty states. He had a way of writing that made you love his laziness, and he loved freedom like I did and basically wandered from town to town, state to state, in search of suds. He'd quit whenever someone pissed him off, or he just felt like it. At some point, Pete gained notoriety, and David Letterman asked him to come on the show. Pete didn't want to do it, so he had his buddy impersonate him. Probably the only time that happened to Letterman! Later, Dave found out about it and finally got the real Dishwasher Pete on the show.

My own dishwashing gig was full of darkness. The vegan food was interesting, the desserts were the best, and my coworkers engaged me a little bit, but I didn't have the camaraderie of climbing to cement too many friendships. There were beautiful women, but it's hard to be the poor dishwasher guy living in a basement with no clue where his life is going, waist deep in suds. That guy isn't going to attract some beautiful woman with direction and light.

At midnight or so, I'd be done with work and I would begin the five-mile bike ride back home. There was a supermarket midway, and, on really cold nights, I would stop there, even if I didn't need anything. Often I would buy nice pens. I couldn't afford anything in the world that was nice, except those pens. I had all different colors and styles, and I would use them to create.

With the help of a random guy I don't remember but I'll never forget, at a Kinko's, I produced my first zine. The owner at the vegan restaurant paid for the printing, and one of the cooks did the cover illustration. I told him one day I was going to be a real writer. He believed me. Sometimes you just have to say your dreams out loud to someone. He offered up a name. "Moonlight Dreamchasers," he said, and added, "Man, I thought of that when I was on mushrooms one night, isn't it good?"

It was. I wrote stories of my climbing, my loneliness and darkness in the city, and even some fiction. I'd never written much fiction before, but the stories I'd hear about Mormon culture made my mind think differently. Whether or not you're Mormon, the influence the church has there is quite powerful. The city is laid out in a grid system that is centered around Temple Square, the Mormon headquarters of the world. The fastest growing and newest large religion in the world is shrouded in mystery. The founder of the church, Joseph Smith, claims to have found golden tablets in New York in the 1820s, and he translated them to create the Book of Mormon. There's no evidence this actually happened, which is enough for a rational person to come to the conclusion that he was insane, but we humans are often not driven by rational thought but rather emotion and sensationalism. Smith also practiced polygamy, and the early Mormon leaders had up to twenty wives each. Driven out of every state they tried to inhabit, they found their home in Utah, before it was even declared a state, and created an empire.

The stories I heard always sounded like fiction. A gay man I worked with, who was a waiter, grew up Mormon, and told me that they would use shock therapy on people who were gay, or the church would hire a prostitute for the man to sleep with in order to cure him. Or, I heard that, in Little Cottonwood Canyon, which boasts exceptional granite climbing, they had a secret hiding area carved out with supplies for the top 144 Mormons if the world fell into disarray. Or, I heard that they had to wear a special kind of undergarment, so, when they died, they would be able to be identified to get into heaven. Seemingly every day, I'd hear some weird stories like these. It was enough to make me not want to be in Salt Lake much longer, but I had no money, and my car was broken down.

One day I received the best possible e-mail I could have ever gotten: the college back in Gunny was looking for a part-time writer, a hired hand paid twenty bucks an hour to write stories and press releases. It was an escape from the prison sentence my life had become. After a month of going back and forth, I got the job. I was moving back home, once and for all.

Chapter 29

The validation that I could be paid to write gave my self-esteem the boost it needed. My parents were proud, and my friends were happy I was coming back to Gunny. Plus, I was relieved to start breathing fresh air again. The smog of Salt Lake got me down, and, unlike most outdoor enthusiasts that live up there, I wasn't escaping to the mountains and canyons to recreate.

I fixed my car, packed it up with everything I owned again, and turned back to the only place I'd ever felt was home in my adult years. It was in the middle of an epic winter, and the whole place was like a snowy, winter wonderland. I was still suffering from tendonitis, and I couldn't really climb, but Ben Johnson showed me a series of exercises I could do to help cure it. And, they worked; by the time spring rolled around, I was back to being a healthy climber.

My job was exactly what I needed at the time. I was in charge of crafting small little pieces that had to be technically proficient. They were often boring, like writing about money for a new building, or a new coach that was brought on board for the failing football team, but it was time to pay my dues if I really wanted to learn the rules of writing. I wore a collared shirt, and every walk I took across our campus was a trip down memory lane. I wondered what my former hippie self would have thought of this guy, who was dressed in button downs and slacks, writing stories for the establishment.

Then, something happened. Two months into the gig, the guy who hired me, and who was in charge of the Public Relations and the Marketing Department, left. He was one year into his job and decided to go back to his old job in Chicago. Just like that, all of a sudden I was the only person in the entire department. They moved me into his office, just down the hall from the president. It was like something out of a movie. Months ago I was hopeless, wondering if my life would be spent washing dishes, living in basements, and writing zines no one would ever read. I was on the fast track to security in the world of a liberal arts higher education. And, that kind of guy is one who will attract a woman with direction and light.

Oh man, I was bullshitting my way through it. I had a degree in Recreation, and everything on my table was writing and marketing related. All kinds of important people would call the office or stop by, and, basically, it was my job to tell them to come back when the new director was hired. Occasionally though, there was a story that just had to be written, or a task that needed to be resolved. I started weekly meetings with the president of the college, a giant of a man, with an equally sized heart and vision that the institution should be a magnificent place of learning and discovery. He was a former professional basketball player in Europe and coached the team at Western from worst in the league to first in the league. I was in awe of his presence and had a nervousness every time we would meet, which kept me on edge. But, we would have these incredible brainstorms. Sometimes a man has a lot to offer simply because of his age and generation. Social media was just getting big, and I explained the world to him. The college was successful in attracting donors and large amounts of money for buildings and scholarships, but their enrollment was declining. He was looking for every angle to put the college on the map. Maybe it was because he had been a pro ball player, and that was my childhood dream, or maybe it was his passion and charisma, but I wanted to do everything in my power to help him achieve his goals for the college.

I was also in charge of writing the alumni magazine. There was a theme for every issue, with profiles of several alums who fit into that theme. They decided the first issue I would write would have the theme of service in the military. I was not psyched. This was still in the end of the George W. Bush years, and I was opposed to the Iraq war that he'd lied to instigate.

In the process of interviewing the people I was assigned to, I realized these were just people like myself, who were assigned to a job. Some were fantastically interesting. One guy worked in the Secret Service and was with President John F. Kennedy when he was assassinated. Another was in between tours in Iraq. War had always seemed distant, but interviewing people who actually went to war was much different. The black and white that college me saw in the world started to fade.

As my life became more routine, more nine to five, I strived to keep my dirtbag self alive. Of course, I was climbing, always climbing. And I was still doing my personal writing. My interest in poetry was renewed. There were many exceptional spoken word poets who were students at the time, and a new level of performance was being reached. We'd all pile into a small venue, like the Gunnison Arts Center, and have performances. Spoken words that you could reach out and feel changed poetry—it made it come alive. Standing on stage and performing a poem I'd practiced a hundred times was an exercise of the mind, and it produced an exhilarating feeling. I kept up with the zines too; no one in Gunnison was producing zines, yet the nature of the creative scene made it ripe for people to be interested. Creativity kept my soul alive as I navigated the landscape of the nine-to-five life.

I was constantly trying to find ways to maintain my spot in the dirtbag culture; I knew I couldn't let it fade, even if I was destined for an office job for the rest of my life, and a wife and kids. That's where it all seemed to be headed. I'd walk across our beautiful campus, and all sorts of nostalgia would build up—the green grass, the large W etched on Tenderfoot Mountain across from campus, the red brick buildings—everything that had built who I was as a person and as someone who found what they needed—to create—was still right at hand. It was as if I just had to dream up what I wanted next, and it would appear.

Of course, the answer was a woman. With all that was going on, my life was still incomplete without a woman. And the quick love, the hookups, were never enough for me, and I would always be paranoid something would go wrong like it did in my younger days. I was only comfortable with love when it was with someone I trusted.

But I walked with a new swagger because I was a writer, and that was the only occupation I ever really wanted to do. I was still making mistakes and learning, and the whole gig was really just like graduate school, a truly higher level of learning, except they were putting money into my bank account, instead of taking it out.

Even though I wasn't getting rich, I was no longer confined to living in a basement or a tent. I still drove that same old Mazda that grew beans in the trunk and took me through some of my best climbing adventures and darkest days. I was still in love with that dirtbag lifestyle—I just had to have some distance, some space from it, in order to love it even more. But I had to proclaim to the world that I was still a part of it; without that, my life was incomplete. And the more I distanced myself from that lifestyle, the more valuable I realized it was, the more important it is to the United States and American culture.

Which is why, a year into my gig, my buddy and I decided to graffiti the Mazda red, white, and blue, with an *om* symbol coming off the hood. We renamed the car The Freedom Mobile. As a suit-and-tie guy, I may have lost all street cred as a dirtbag, but, when I clocked out and hit the road, The Freedom Mobile helped me retain my status. Freedom, as we called the car for short, made women smile and children dance with joy. She was beautiful.

At the college, I was immediately a peer with my former professors. I was a difficult student to say the least, always have been, from my early days up until the day I finally graduated; half of it was me wanting to challenge the system, the other half just simply being a stubborn pain in the ass. I'd have to collaborate with teachers I'd pissed off and questioned in their classrooms. I also crossed paths with the professor who gave me the only F I'd ever received in my life, in the Bob Dylan course. One day at a poetry event, we were joking about it, and I said the line I'd always say when reminiscing about the class with someone, "I think Bob Dylan would be proud."

Without hesitation he replied with his Southern drawl and a wise smile, "I think you're right."

When a man reaches this point in life, approaching thirty and still single, and doesn't want to be single, at every social event there's an underlying purpose—to meet someone. And, it goes beyond someone to share a night or two with; it's looking for someone to maybe share the rest of your life with. All of the other parts were set: I had a job, a home I loved, cold as it was, and I had confidence.

So I looked and looked and sometimes the too much looking leads to nothing, because you're looking too much. My first couple years back, I was indeed that guy. Plus, Gunny isn't exactly a hub for single, good looking young adults—it's a small college town where most people move on to bigger and better after college.

At night, I'd walk across campus to go home and be alone, and there would still be lights on in the offices, and I wondered if my love was in one of those offices? If she was a lonely professor too, looking for someone to keep her warm? And was she the future mother of my children, my life partner that I would grow old with in this comfortable but cold remote corner of Colorado?

After two cold winters with no one to keep me warm, and spring on the way, the old familiar Gunnison angst was getting to me. The fall before, I'd indeed met a professor that I'd proclaimed my affections for, but she had a boyfriend back East and turned away my efforts for reciprocation. I was going crazy on the inside but outwardly retained my collared-shirt-and-slacks cool. And, of course, The Freedom Mobile let me retain my cool when I was out and about on the great American road.

I learned some things though, lonely as I was, I could still focus and have purpose. I learned a little trick about writing, which in turn made me realize just how slow of a learner I was: In order to be a writer you must write. You must write in a routine, I think, unless you're the Hunter S. Thompson Gonzo drug type, but that path never worked for me. I could barely spell my name or hold a conversation on drugs, let alone write a masterpiece. Five to seven days a week, depending on how much I was climbing, I was writing. The pathways in my brain became more connected to the process, and it got easier and easier as time went by. Before, I'd simply liked the outlet, the idea of being a writer, but once I was writing all the time, I realized it's this blue-collar thing—roll your sleeves up and get the work done. That's not all of it; maybe it was all of it for the press release, boring, matter of fact type writing, but for the creative stuff, it was all in. The discipline, the magic, and relating an actual experience, when those all came together, well, it was like magic.

And my climbing, I realized I didn't need to live it 24/7 to hang on to my abilities. If anything, the full-on climber life was holding me back, stealing the magic from it. When I had only a few hours to climb, or just the weekend, I was so much more in the moment. I also started to cross train, to diversify, and started mountain biking and running more. Something was especially Zen about trail running, another key to unlocking the endurance puzzle.

Running was how I got her. Or maybe she was trying to get me? The professor, Lynn, who I was chasing, shot me down, so I forgot about her, or at least I tried as much as I could, but then, in the peak of the spring, when Gunnison is finally released from the clutches of winter, she reached out to me. It was just for drinks with friends, and I was hesitant at first, my guarded heart protecting me. But you should never let your heart fully be protected; after all, the heart holds the key to everything.

With a simple touch, a reaching out, it was all over, rather it was all on—I had a lady. Lynn was touched by my gesture of telling my feelings for her in the autumn, she just could not reciprocate. She broke up with the "back East" boyfriend shortly after, but she was heartbroken and needed to mend. The winter seemed to do that for her, and she was ready to love again. And, so was I.

We recreated in the lands of Gunnison, running, biking, and climbing, all part of the process in courting a beautiful woman in a beautiful land. She had striking dark hair, long legs, and a vibrant energy. She had an adorable golden retriever I loved instantly. The stairs to her bedroom were like a short climb to a release and a level of intimacy I'd been trying to reach for some time now.

•All the cards were on the table instantly. She had her own epic of sadness from a previous relationship gone wrong. I told her of mine. I don't know if it is just a sad world out there, but so many of the women I'd dated in the past had something very sad and wrong happen to them. Some had been raped. Lynn had a former lover try to kill her. It was very traumatic, and she was very guarded when she told me. It didn't bother me one bit. I'd made so many mistakes in my life it was oddly comforting to hear her own tale of survival and moving on from such trauma.

Right off the bat, another card was on the table—she had taken a job back East to be a professor there. She accepted the job with plans to continue with "the boyfriend," but he broke up with her anyways after she took the position. I was used to being transient and living in the moment; it hardly affected my feelings for her. I also had a problem with vision, planning my life ahead of time.

So we lay together under the cover of love for many hours, becoming days, weeks, months. All I really wanted to do was get to know her and make love to her and live under this cover of love. She lived in a house all by herself, and we had nothing in the world to stop us.

We traveled to hot springs and bathed naked under the azure of the sky, our bodies glistening in the sun. We made love in a tent. I could hardly keep up with her; men, we are the aggressors, going in for the hunt, the kill, but there is no kill in love, at least not when you're making it. The sex drive of a woman is much more infinite than the man's—we come out charging, she plays coy and pushes away but then comes back with a fury. I loved that fury and tried to keep up. It was a joy of exhaustion.

My work life did not match the joy of my love life, other than the constant change that is all life. The president had a stroke and nearly died. I was given another boss, a new person to report to. She knew nothing of mountain culture and was all business, and she was a bad businessperson. She might as well have been the Wicked Witch of the West. She and I did not connect, to say the least. She knew nothing about the mountains. Her hero was Bobby Knight, the old basketball coach famous for his temper and throwing chairs onto the court when he was angry. Change was brewing. Lynn saw the same thing in my new boss; they would be in the same meetings sometimes, and we made fun of her together.

In the midst of making love one night, I told Lynn I loved her. I'd never told another lover that before. I guess I was waiting. Thirty fucking years old and I'd never done that. The game of love can be a slow play, that's for sure.

I was in love with her, and I did my best to not stray from the moment. Then, all of a sudden, talks and plans were made. She was moving and I was staying. Or was I? I started to entertain the idea. I looked at the place in Pennsylvania where she would be teaching. How far was it from climbing? Far. How important was my lifestyle out in Gunny? It was everything. But, how important was love? Love was everything too.

Sometimes I go back and think of that woman, that house, that period of time. The stage was set for a happy but domesticated life. I had a steady job with a good paycheck and benefits. The only thing missing was a family, and a beautiful woman is where I had to begin. And, I never would have got the girl if I were a depressed guy living in a basement and washing dishes. Maybe I was just coming into my own, or maybe I was just finally making some good decisions? Eventually I had to really start thinking; the girl was about to slip through my hands and be a thousand miles away, on the wrong side of the country for a guy like me.

In the midst of all of this was the downturn in the economy. The college was receiving less of a budget than the previous year, and everyone was worried about what might happen to them. I was initially worried, but, taking stock of my job, I realized my greatest days might be behind me there: the president, whom I admired so much, was no longer my boss, and he was still recovering from a stroke—he could no longer look after me and be my mentor. And, I had no respect or motivation coming from my new boss. Secretly I was hoping my job would be in jeopardy. Also, I was tired of the meetings, the politics, and the formalities. The honeymoon was over.

When the budget for the next year came in, it was announced my position would be cut to half time. Outwardly, I was disappointed—after all, I'd worked so hard to get to where I was, and now it seemed like I'd worked so much for nothing. Inside, the dirtbag in me saw that I would have more freedom. I would only have to be at the office twenty hours a week.

The honeymoon had just begun with Lynn, only a few months into it, and her upcoming move stared us in the face. I don't think either one of us wanted to think about it; we just continued to live and love together. We planned a trip right before she was going to move. We would go to Boulder together for a wedding, then go out to Yosemite, where we could bask in some final days of her time out West.

Weddings bring up some crazy energy. We all think about the love being shared with the two people who get married, but we also think about our own lives. This wedding was small and felt a little sad. The bride was upset that people couldn't make it, and I heard her openly complain about that to Lynn. Lynn had nothing but loyalty running through her veins and was a good friend. There was a lot of down time at this wedding without alcohol, and I was restless and bored. I texted my old college friend Mark, who was now living in Yosemite, about how boring the wedding was. Lynn looked over my shoulder and read the text and was upset with me.

It should have been a perfect night; we were living a great love affair in Boulder, a perfect place for romance, and we had an exquisite hotel room booked for the night, right downtown. Everything was bubbling to the surface though. All I could think about was that, if I wanted this to continue, I'd have to move back to the flatlands, to the East Coast. I did want it to continue. I did not want to move to Pennsylvania.

In the hotel room that night, we broke up. I lamented about how I could not move east. She cried, and I felt horribly guilty. We made love that night, but without the love. We were both holding onto what was now the past. Then, the next morning, without much thought, we got in her car and drove to Yosemite.

The tension in the car was thick. There was always an uncertainty when I went to Yosemite. Some travel to the accessible big wall Mecca of the world and never make it back, lives lost to the pursuit of climbing. That was always in the back of my mind. This time it was different. I was about to lose love.

We stopped in Salt Lake City to spend the night. We stayed at Adam's place even though he wasn't there; he was off having some adventure. Another day of driving, and we arrived in Yosemite.

Mark and Scott, who were roommates all throughout college, both ended up in Yosemite. We joked that they were heterosexual life partners. Scott was living at this place called The Green House, a perfect little old school cabin, set on the edge of the Big Meadow, just ten minutes from the Valley floor in the little community of Foresta. If you hiked up on a small hill, you could see the very top of El Capitan poking out. It was my favorite little house in the world.

I always made sure I got out to Yosemite for at least one week every year when I was working this nine-to-five life. It was usually this time of year, before college started back up, and I could escape. It wasn't ideal; Yosemite was still in the grips of summer, and it was quite warm. Staying at the Green House was ideal though—no pesky rangers bothering you like they do in Camp 4, and the life there was so energetic and relaxing. It was my happy place.

The year before, Mark was housesitting for Scott, and I fell in love. I fell in love with this place. In crowded, big Yosemite, who knew there was such a place of tranquility and peace so close? The meadow, living up to its name, the Big Meadow, stretched for as far as the eye could see with only a couple big barns next to the house, and that was it. The house originally was home to a family of farmers, who lived there when a railroad went right by. Now the house was home to two lucky environmental educators, who usually lived there for a year or two and then moved on. It was a golden moment to have Scott living there.

With all the simple beauty, there was a tragedy that occurred that you simply had to know about if you spent any time at the Green House. Mark told me solemnly one day, "There was a murder here."

It was a brutal and terrible killing, on a day like any day I spent there, a summer day. Joie Armstrong, an environmental educator, just like Scott, was killed during the summer of 1999, by a man who had already committed several other murders that year. I found out a few days into my time there, and I felt the profound sadness, even though I didn't know the woman—the peace that existed in that space was stolen from someone. There was a little gravestone on the property by some apple trees. I walked over one day to pay tribute and clean it off a little bit. There was a journal at the house that dated all the way back to when the murder happened, and I read many entries by a man that had spent a lot of time at the Green House, who knew Joie and was getting over her loss. Throughout the years, there were entries by people that had passed through. I loved that stuff, and, after fifty-one weeks of being in an office and staring at a computer screen, sitting in a little rustic house and reading and writing was the perfect remedy. I cried for Joie, more than I ever had for a stranger, much less one who died over a decade ago.

The summer of 1999 meant so much to me because it was the summer I took off from home and almost ended it all. How sad and how grateful I was that I did not take my own life, or have some accident when I was so carelessly and so hopelessly driving the highways of America.

The sadness of this love affair between Lynn and I ending hung in the air during this visit so much that I was unable to access the meditation and peace that I felt the year before. Lynn met Mark and his wife Norma, and I'd been excited about them meeting, but we were no longer a couple, so what was there to be excited about? I learned that Scott had just broken up with his girlfriend as well, and he was even more down and out than I was.

We set a little tent up in the big meadow. The year before, I stayed in the same place by myself and wished for a woman's company. Now I had it, but the stars were not aligned. Timing is everything, and the timing was off. The magic was leaving us too. We held on and made love in that meadow under the blanket of the stars and on the bed of Mother Nature, but whatever we had that was so good was leaving us. I had yet to begin processing it all. Instead of dealing with this failing relationship, I was dreaming of climbing again. After all, I was in Yosemite.

We wanted our connection to last and held on as long as we could, but reality hit, and we started to bicker. She decided to spend the night away from me with a friend who was a park ranger there. Then the next day when I returned to the Green House after some cragging, there was a small pile of my clothes and a note saying I needed to call her. I did, and she had made up her mind that she needed to leave. As we talked, and she cried, I walked outside the Green House. The sun was setting, and it was the most dramatic orange my eyes had ever seen, like an answer. Lynn asked me if I wanted to go back with her. I had only a few vacation days left, and here was the first woman I'd ever truly fallen in love with, slipping away from my life. Do I hold on and change my ways? Reach out to her and tell her our love means too much, and I'll do anything to make it work? A better, stronger man might have. Or, a man that is not so fickle and dependent on climbing and the wild to be happy. I made the decision to stay in Yosemite. Immediately, I felt free. Lynn was gone, and all I had to think about now was climbing. Ignorance is bliss.

Freedom, there's a lot of talk about it here in these United States. We all love freedom, all human beings love freedom, all breathing creatures do. This newfound freedom I was basking in was a false feeling. I had lost love, and that feeling doesn't sink in right away. I guess its also called denial. The next day Scott and I went big, climbing the notoriously runout Stoner's Highway, the perfect recipe to clear the mind and live in the moment.

I figured that it would be just a regular outing on the rock that would pose only minor difficulties given the 5.10 rating and the fact that I've been climbing at the grade for ten years.

We jokingly dubbed ourselves "Team Breakup" while hiking up the trail to the wall. I was more than eager to do some longer climbing; we'd been festering around the short, one-pitch, well-traveled climbs for the last few days, and I had the itch to get a few hundred feet off the ground. With a game of rock, paper, scissors, it was decided that I would start out with the leading; an easy but loose and crumbly pitch led us up to the beginning of the more difficult climbing.

I've always found that when space is gained into the vertical, above the ground, my headspace becomes different as well. Reflection is natural when looking around you in the vertical world, and in nature. That day, my thoughts were with Lynn; they were thoughts of guilt. I'd led her all the way out to Yosemite to realize that my own selfishness was at the heart of the journey. I wanted to experience being up high on the walls, and she was a beginner, and we were broken up. How did everything happen so fast?

The meditation and reflection of hanging on the wall is gained through climbing. This day the climbing demanded some serious focus, much more than I had anticipated. After my first mellow lead, it was Scott's turn on the sharp end of the rope. I watched him climb twenty-five feet to my left, with no gear off the belay. Had he fallen, he would have violently come swinging back my way. So falling wasn't an option. Scott brilliantly completed the sequence, secured more gear, and then climbed another runout section. He arrived at the belay, and then I cleaned the pitch, and soon it was my turn for a runout lead.

Scott had set the tone with his incredible, delicate climbing, and I was determined to emulate his style. I climbed up off the belay about five feet, clipped a piton, a relic from the seventies, all rusted, a "maybe" piece of protection, as in, if you fall, maybe it will hold. Then I climbed twenty feet out to the left, heading for a crack system. At this point, I was on a small perch, contemplating my fall, with my toes on some good footholds and my hands on some decent holds as well, eyeing the next moves to get to where I could place some pro in a crack that would hold a fall. It's at this point in climbing where complete focus is necessary. I zoned in to the moment, delicately stepped up, eyeing a handhold, leaned into it, and stepped up to where I could place some gear. I was safe again and climbed up a decently protected crack system to the next belay.

Stoner's Highway demanded this type of dangerous, delicate, in-the-moment type of climbing, pitch after pitch. Scott seemed to get the most difficult pitches, with thirty and even forty-foot runouts on 5.10 climbing. He told me he didn't think he could have done the moves if he hadn't just broken up with his girlfriend and was in the state of mind he was in. I don't think my breakup figured into my risk taking. I just wanted to be up climbing on the wall with a friend and reflect.

We made it up to the ninth pitch, and it was my turn to lead. The first bolt was a good twenty feet up above the belay, and I couldn't confidently reach it. I climbed back down to Scott, and he went up. He felt the same about the risk—it was too much. We rappelled back to the ground.

Rappelling is usually the scary part, but this time there was relief in the air. We didn't complete Stoner's Highway, but we'd done enough mind-clearing and thought-provoking climbing that I felt the same piece of mind I get after doing a big trad climb. That clarity of being in the moment, the feeling that life is one crazy ride and you just have to roll with the punches, know when to fight and when to run away. We ended up running away on Stoner's Highway, and we never came back; speaking for myself, I don't know if I could ever get the nerve to go back. But it was the perfect climb for that moment of recklessness, that feeling of abruptness a breakup can induce. And we both had the satisfaction that we didn't give in to the craziness and believe that we could do something dangerous that we shouldn't have done. The closure of that breakup didn't come for months, even years, but I had clarity.

After this, maybe the best thing would have been to do a big wall, completely leave the horizontal for a few days, leave this old, tired, sad world behind. But I was still an office jock, and I was expected back at the college in just a few days. That meant I had only one more big day-climb left. I suggested Astroman, and Mark obliged. He'd already done it, and, after the runout head games I'd played on Stoner's Highway, I knew I was ready to face this climb.

Astroman had the reputation—it was a benchmark climb, and she was a beauty. Named after a Jimi Hendrix song and established by John Long, John Bachar, and Ron Kauk, three Yosemite legends, the climb was one I thought might usher my abilities into another level. It wasn't. Stoner's Highway was logistically more difficult, but Astroman was a perfect work of art, some of the finest cracks and corners I'd ever climbed. That day my goal was to forget about Lynn, pushing those thoughts back to some place in my mind.

After Astroman, I had to find a way home quickly. I was expected back at work in just a couple days. Fortunately, an old college buddy, Tory, had just finished film school at UCLA and was planning on heading back to Gunny for the rest of the summer. All I had to do was take a bus to Los Angeles, and he would give me a ride.

I don't know when it all hit me, maybe the endless desert of Utah, or maybe just when we crossed back into Colorado and saw that Welcome to Colorado sign, but I'd left home with a woman I thought I might spend the rest of my life with and came home without her, and she would never be in my life again.

She was around Gunny for another week before she left for the East Coast. When I saw her around town, it was the strangest thing because we had nothing to share anymore except the past. I went over and exchanged belongings, probably some books or something, maybe music, who knows, I don't remember what, but I remember that setting. It was raining and her dog, the sweet golden retriever, was confused by the boxes and the moving, and why I wasn't around anymore. I don't even remember what we said; I just remember that dog expressed the sadness better than I could.

When she left, it sank in. My job became a mess too. Reduced to half time, I didn't know what to cut out and what to do. When I was full time I was supposed to work forty hours a week, but anyone at a small organization knows that is never the case. I was working way more than forty hours and had built tight relationships. Now, I had to say no a lot to people who were used to me delivering. One day, I learned about the budget and how my job could have been saved, but my supervisor didn't allocate the funds to do so. That was it, I decided—I was done.

I'd also gone back to washing dishes part time to pay the bills, back to the same job in Crested Butte I'd done off and on for ten years. My mentor there, the kitchen manager, was always warning me not to get stuck in that line of work, to make something better of myself, to build for the future. We talked about writing all the time, and he encouraged me to purse that path. He was a vagabond dirtbag like me and lived through the sixties and all that. He would live in a tent, even in the winter, and had just settled out of that life as he closed in on fifty years old. He had a son he never saw, and I think in some ways our friendship helped him with that. His voice was always in the back of my head, and I felt like I'd let him down.

I was going crazy, and there was no flow to my existence. I needed out, again, but what was I to do? The economy was at an all-time low, and I was still blessed enough to have some work; I still had all my benefits at the college. A reasonable man would have stuck it out. I was looking for an escape plan that would lead me away from this situation as soon as possible.

I don't know where the idea came from, probably just looking at a road map, old school style, but I decided I might want to move down south, to Durango, in a little corner of the Southwest, right next to where the four corners of Colorado, Utah, New Mexico, and Arizona meet. I started sending out e-mails to various contacts at the local papers and the college there, and I made a quick trip down to visit.

One cup of coffee can change your life. I drove the Freedom Mobile down, blazing through some of the craziest mountain passes in Colorado through the San Juan Mountains, to meet the editor of the *Durango Telegraph*, the weekly independent paper there. We had a mutual contact through the Gunnison paper, and he casually said, sure, you can write for us. It was like a hundred bucks a story, but it was a lead, it was something. I decided right then and there that I'd move to this town where I'd spent a total of an hour of my life. I zipped Freedom back up to Gunny and told all my friends I was leaving. My old college friend Shaun, who had just returned there after living in New York City for three years and doing the corporate thing, told me I needed to have some goals, have a plan. What was my plan? I didn't have a plan; I just had to get out of town.

I met with the president of the college and told him about my plans to leave. He was dealing with all kinds of woes at the college, mostly resulting from the downturn in the economy, and my departure seemed to just be one more thing. I transitioned out of my job and tried to reach out for things that would keep me sane. Dave and I climbed the Painted Wall in the Black Canyon—at 2,300 feet, it's the tallest cliff in Colorado. We accidently spent the night on the wall and cuddled together for warmth. We suffered incredibly, but it energized me and gave me hope, in some weird way.

After I left my job, I had a few weeks open. It was mid-October, so there wasn't much work to be had washing dishes in Crested Butte, and I got lazy. I made the final plans for my departure.

In three years, I accumulated more possessions than would fit in my car—breaking the dirtbag golden rule. It took days and days to get rid of everything I didn't need: the TV, the bed, the furniture, the microwave, the plates and forks and knives and cleaning products, all those things you just don't need when you don't know where you'll live next.

My plan was to travel and climb for a month, then circle back down to Durango and move there for good. I'd lined up a partner, Gene, and we agreed that we'd take his truck. A week later, the truck's engine blew up. We had two options: take the Freedom Mobile, or not do the trip at all. Of course, we rolled the dice and put Freedom on the road.

I put everything I owned into the Freedom Mobile. The day before I left was all gray, imminent winter on the way. I'd been renting an apartment from my college writing mentor, George Sibley, and, just

before I left, we had a little conversation.

Like many great writers, and George is a great writer if there ever was one, he is a simple man of words in conversation. Now in his seventies, George has seen it all. He'd married once, had children, divorced, and then didn't find his second wife until his fifties. He knew what I was chasing, and the present situation could have been summed up with one look at this graffitied red, white, and blue car.

He noted that the Freedom Mobile was weighted down so bad the back shocks were almost touching the tire. This was a big bet I was waging. What if this thing broke down ten miles outside of Gunny? What was the plan then? I hardly had any money in my bank account. The goal that day was just to simply get to Telluride, where Gene was. If I could do that, I was gone from Gunny. Forever.

Chapter 30

I was full of worry in the weeks leading up to the departure. I was worried about money. I was worried about the future. I was worried about the upcoming road trip and worried about how long it would be before I met another woman that could live up to the standards Lynn had set. I was a mess. The minute I set off on the road I could only pick one worry and stick with it, and that worry was getting Freedom to the next destination. I was a road warrior again.

The Freedom Mobile was running, but barely. Seven out of the nine dashboard warning lights were on, and the headlights only worked when I popped the hood and fiddled with some wires. And we were going to take this thing to Las Vegas, and then to California, and then back to Colorado?

Sure enough, the car made it to Telluride, and we liquidated everything that we wouldn't need for the trip into Gene's garage. Gene was dealing with a breakup as well, and we both just wanted to see the open road and warm rocks to climb. We wasted no time, and that next morning we were Vegas bound.

If you could picture this old car, worth only a few hundred bucks, rolling into Las Vegas at night, in film, it would be something spectacular to see. The land of sin and money, America's excess spilling over into this sad desert city, all lit up, the Freedom Mobile providing the perfect contrast, the truth of America, all beat up, but somehow still running, somehow still on the road.

It was nothing but sunshine in Las Vegas, and we climbed for a few days until we headed down south, back to Joshua Tree, and then up to Yosemite. In J-Tree, I got a call from an elderly couple in Durango, looking for someone to look after their house for the winter. They'd found an ad I'd placed in the newspaper that I was going to write for. It was perfect, one less thing for my worried mind to be preoccupied with. At least I had a start, a new foundation— when you're a climber out on the road, you never know if you might just stay on the road forever.

The Freedom Mobile still had the check engine light on, but it continued to float on down the highway, so we just kept rolling. It was a funky little highway out of Joshua Tree that led us to the interstate, one of those interstates where you can see the smog from miles away and sense the gloom of it all.

It was this sort of highway that carried us to Yosemite, the big wall Mecca of the world. Gene and I bought two weeks of groceries, stuffing the Freedom Mobile to the brim with the type of supplies that one needs for big wall climbing: canned food, coffee, granola bars, and gas for the stove. We rolled into the park late, haggard from the road, and headed straight to the Green House.

As we got out of the Freedom Mobile, we noticed the air was unexpectedly warm for November in Yosemite. The Green House was more than welcoming, as always. In the living room were Scott and his roommate Ned, and two of their friends, fellow climbers, destined to be our friends as well. We cracked beers and toasted to the possibility of good climbing weather in November.

Gene and I were set on climbing El Capitan. Neither of us had climbed it before, and we thought that this was the trip. In the morning, over coffee, we decided that we would start up the wall the following day.

Driving into the Valley that morning, we met up with Mark. He was finishing up his season as the Valley was slowing down with winter on its way. We mentioned that we were going to start up the Nose on El Capitan the following day, and he asked if he could join. Mark has made several trips up The Captain, and he is a fun and energetic guy; we didn't mind at all if he joined.

Immediately, we noticed that Mark's demeanor was erratic. First he could go, and then he could not. He was busy moving out of his place for the season, and he seemed to have a lot on his mind. To make matters more complicated, Scott called and said he would like to join us as well.

That afternoon, while Scott was working and Mark was busy with errands, Gene and I went to the El Capitan meadow, just to stare at it and see how many climbers were on the 3,000 foot wall. Incredibly, we could only see one solo climber, high on the Nose. It was a great feeling to know we would finally be climbing on El

Capitan the following day.

The first time I saw El Capitan, it seemed so big, so improbable to want to climb it. Now, finally, after honing our skills for years and years, it was time to try to climb The Big Stone. I was full of confidence and motivation. My recent climb of the Painted Wall in the Black Canyon had me convinced that I could now climb El Cap. After all, if I had the skills to get up the biggest cliff in Colorado, I could get up the tallest one in California, right?

"Gene, maybe after we climb the Nose we could do the Salathe Wall. It would be really cool to climb it twice, don't you think?" I said.

Gene mumbled something at the ridiculous ambition of my comment, and we continued to tilt our necks back, looking up at over 3,000 feet of sheer, golden granite.

We went back to the Green House to pack up for the climb. It was hectic. I wasn't happy that we were, all of a sudden, a team of four. But, plans kept changing throughout the day, so I knew there was a chance that something would happen and things would change again.

We laid out a tarp and stuffed two big haul bags, nearly the size of a man and almost the weight of one. Mark continued to be frantic, "So there is a chance I have to work. If so, I'll just rappel off with an extra rope."

Mark's demeanor didn't get me psyched, and I made subtle hints about how a team of four might be too much. We were hungry for the big wall experience, and Mark was clearly low on excitement for it. He'd been living and working in Yosemite for almost six months and didn't have the fire. I was beginning to think he just wanted to hang out with us, and this was how he was going about it.

Mark is one of my best friends—no, Mark is like a brother that shares the love of climbing—so I just put my head down and continued to pack up. Scott finally showed up and confirmed that he was in. He laid out his gear on the gigantic tarps and started stuffing it in.

By this time it was dark, and we had moved inside the Green House and were still packing. In addition to this, we were drinking and smoking and getting weary. Scott's roommate Ned, a big wall veteran himself, just looked at us and could sense the madness and the confusion.

Finally, near the end of the packing, Mark quickly reached into the haul bag to find something, accidentally pulled out a carabiner, which smacked him in the face, knocking out half of one of his front teeth. Suddenly it was quiet. Scott whispered what we were all thinking, that Mark would not be coming up the wall. He would have to visit a dentist in the morning. He was bummed but stayed in good spirits. Mark started removing his gear from the bags. Late in the night, I crawled into my tent for a few hours of sleep. I set my alarm for 4:20 a.m.

The alarm went off, and I felt tired. Like a true fiend, I headed straight inside to get coffee going. The coffee ignited the fire of my determination, and I felt motivated. Gene made up some grub, and we packed the two large haul bags into the Freedom Mobile.

It was still dark as we drove from Foresta into the Valley. We parked the Freedom Mobile by the El Cap meadow and made the short approach to the wall. After the coffee wore off, I felt tired, and the task of humping our gear to El Cap, while short, was draining. I looked at Gene, with the haul bag on his back, and he was sweating heavily. Scott, on the other hand, seemed to be in his element, accepting all of these struggles as part of the game.

Since Scott was the aid-climbing expert, it was agreed that he would lead the first block of pitches. He started up, moving quickly, and then commenced the hauling of the bags. They didn't budge on the slab, and Gene had to push them up to get started. At that moment, Gene and I knew we were in for some serious suffering and hard work, and we looked at each other.

"You know," I said, "we probably should have done a practice aid wall before jumping on El Cap." He looked back and agreed, with the ocean of golden granite towering above us.

Finally, Gene had to jumar up to assist Scott with the hauling, as they both grunted and struggled to move the haul bags inches. I jumared up as well and thought about the time that had passed since we'd started the pitch. When we reached the second pitch, well over two hours had passed, and I thought of how daring, expert big wall Yosemite climbers had speed climbed the entire route in the time it took us to get up the first two hundred feet.

The suffering and turmoil got worse as the morning progressed and turned into the afternoon. There were traversing pitches where I had to lower out the two haul bags so that Scott and Gene could haul. I'd never done this, and the weight of the bags pulled terrifyingly on me. I was to the point of cursing and complaining already. But, a party was behind us, and a woman was leading up behind me, and there was no way I was about to have a meltdown in front of another climber, a female one at that, just a few pitches up on El Cap.

The woman arrived at my belay as I struggled with the haul bags, and she clipped into the same bolted anchor I was using. She and her partner were only doing the initial pitches of the climb and so were equipped with a light free-climbing rack and nothing else, the same style that the speed climbing aces use to run up the wall in a few hours.

They looked so free and happy. I was having problems un-weighting the haul bag from the anchor, and the woman helped me get the weight of the bags off the anchor by pushing up on them, so they could be lowered out with the remaining rope. "How far are you all going today?" she asked.

"Uh, I think we need to go back to the drawing board, maybe go do a shorter aid route," I replied. I was already coming to the realization that Gene and I had a lot to learn about big wall aid climbing before trying to climb El Cap.

At this ledge, I thought about style and hated that we had so much weight, and it was such a task to haul all the supplies up. I thought about how we had come all the way out to Yosemite just to suffer like this, because, after all, even if we did not realize it at the time, we were doing exactly what we'd come to do. To learn to big wall aid climb is to suffer, and then, after that suffering, the knowledge is attained and the rewards are found.

Finally, Scott and Gene began the hauling, and I started up the pitch. There was a traversing section where I had to lower myself out with the extra rope that was dangling off my harness. I'd never done this before and was terrified. Scott, just forty feet above, was close enough that he could offer a tutorial on how it was done. I finally lowered myself out, and, like many climbing procedures, it was not as scary as the initial perception in my head. We were lucky to have Scott on board, and, if Mark were there, he could have provided beneficial lessons as well. Gene and I had a lot to learn.

When I arrived at the belay with Scott and Gene, we had an enormous eruption of laughter at our struggle. I couldn't recall the last time I laughed that hard, and I felt a weight off my shoulders as I laughed to the point of tears.

We were at a spot where we could rappel down directly in a short amount of time, so we debated what we were going to do. Scott was game to continue, and I think Gene could have gone either way. I'd made my mind up at the last belay that I wanted to hone my skills some more before climbing The Captain. I expressed this to my friends, and they obliged to retreat. Sometimes, admitting failure can be a blow to a climber's ego, but, at that point, I had no ego to blow. I imagined I was the worst aid climber in Yosemite, and I didn't give a damn, which, in itself, was a relief and a revelation. Freedom's just another word for nothin' left to lose, right?

Retreat was not as easy as we imagined. At that point, there were now five climbers at the belay ledge, us and the other party. There wasn't any tension though, which can happen at a crowded belay ledge, especially with failure in the air. We were sitting there trying to figure out how to rappel off with the mighty haul bags the weight of a man. The woman's partner, a big wall veteran himself, originally from Alabama, who'd already been up El Capitan and all the other walls in Yosemite, advised us to simply lower the bags off as one of us rappelled down and clipped the bag into the next anchor. He was right; it was the most efficient way to do it, rather than having one of us rappel with the bags attached to us and fumble down the wall. As we messed with the bags, he was hilarious.

At one point, Scott had the bags in between his legs, and the guy joked, "I bet you always wanted to ride a fat chick, huh?" in a way that only a Southerner could say.

We talked to him more as Scott rappelled down. "Oh man you guys are trying El Cap for your first big wall in Yosemite? That's ambitious. I did five or six practice walls before getting on this thing. Almost died once of heatstroke on the Leaning Tower, trying to climb it in the summer, we were so stupid..." He went on with his stories. Big wall climbers all have these stories, and it's more proof in my mind that every big wall climber suffers for every bit of glory attained.

I was feeling glorious and relieved when we finally touched back on the ground. It wasn't the goal—the goal was to top out on El Cap, three or so days later, but I'd learned some valuable lessons. Gene and I talked it over, and we would take a rest day, repack, and then attempt a shorter big wall route.

The weather was still sunny and warm, blue skies and all, a blessing for early November. Mark wanted to do some sport climbing, so we met up with him in the early afternoon the next day. Sport climbing is somewhat of a rarity for Yosemite, which is traditional in its nature.

We hiked up to some obscure wall for a couple routes. The trees were changing colors, the gigantic Yosemite Falls still had some water flowing down it, and we even had a bear leisurely stroll by in the forest below us.

Mark was loving it. He was over the suffering of big walls and just wanted to bask in the simple play that is sport climbing. He made us laugh as he jokingly used his new kneepads that he was going to use for overhanging sport climbing in Mexico, where he lives and works in the winter with his girlfriend.

That night, we packed up the haul bag, one haul bag, because it was just going to be Gene and me for the climb. We decided to go for the all time beginner's classic, the South Face of the Washington Column, a thousand-plus-foot wall of mostly straightforward aid climbing. Gene and I both had failed previously on this route, so there was also the prospect of redemption, something that always sweetens the deal when figuring out what to climb. I'd also done the classic free climb, Astroman, on the same wall, with Mark the previous summer, in nine hours, which gave me confidence that we could get up the South Face in two days, even with all the extra baggage for living and sleeping on the wall.

There was an air of calm as we packed up the bag in the Green House. Ned and Scott watched us pack. Scott talked of plans to do a climb nearby to ours, Southern Man, with another climbing partner on our second day, so it would be a party on the wall. We continued to pack and organize late in the night, and Ned stayed up with us, saying he wanted to be part of the excitement. He commented that he could sense we were going to be successful this time, and I took that to be a blessing and a good sign.

We woke up around 4:20 again, completed the ritual of drinking coffee, eating, and pooping, and made our way into the Valley in the dark. Funny thing about climbing the Washington Column, one parks his car in the parking lot for the upscale Ahwahnee Hotel; it's an atrocity, if you ask me, that there is a luxurious hotel in a National park dedicated to preserving a natural environment. I say tear it down and build more campsites and housing for the park employees, who, for the most part, live in small, uncomfortable quarters. Regardless, it felt strange as we parked the Freedom Mobile next to all the nice BMWs, Hummers, and other vehicles for rich folk, pulled the haul bag out of the car, and started hiking up to the wall.

As we were getting our gear together, we noticed another duo doing exactly what we were doing. Since the South Face is so popular, we figured they were getting on the same route we were. We weren't exactly psyched on the prospect of getting stuck behind another party, so we tried to get our act together and started hiking to the wall. I led us astray at one point, hiking past the trailhead that heads up to the Washington Column, but luckily we got to the base of the route just before the other party, again, possibility for tension as they arrived just five minutes after we had. The first thing they said was, "I hope you boys are ready to party on the ledge. We got some whiskey." Both Gene and I were relieved that they weren't going to be impatient with us.

The South Face of the Washington Column is a genius route to get acclimated on the rituals and mechanisms of big wall climbing, provided it's not a traffic jam of climbers. One can climb the wall with only hauling the bag for three pitches up to Dinner Ledge, leaving them there after spending the night on the ledge, climbing to the top of the wall, and then rappelling back to the bag, much lighter after two days, and finally rappelling with the bag back to the ground.

We fought and struggled with the haul bag for three pitches, maybe four hundred feet or so, cursing and sweating, till we finally reached Dinner Ledge, a urine smelling but glorious place to be. We basically collapsed on the ledge for a while. After resting for a bit, we began laying out our sleeping territory and taking our stove and food out of the haul bag along with all the other little comforts we had to set ourselves up to enjoy a night on the wall.

Our new friends, Ben and Patrick, progressed below us at about the same pace we did, and we exchanged friendly remarks to one another as they came up to the ledge. They were able to find their own little perch to sleep on, just five feet higher and thirty or so feet adjacent to our own little camp.

Once camp was set up and our bodies were energized, we did another couple pitches. I led, as we were doing the climbing in blocks, and, on the second pitch, I started to feel comfortable in the environment. I'd been here before. Half Dome, to the east, stood proudly, looking over us and seeming to give us its blessing. The aid-climbing movement, stepping in our ladder-like sling aiders, much different than the progress of free climbing, using only one's hands and feet, finally felt right and efficient. On the last pitch of the day, I was truly feeling a flow on the golden-granite wall. I moved quickly, and Gene made positive remarks about my progress, which made me feel good. There was a small, easy pendulum, which I completed, gently swinging over, and I felt like a child lost in play. I clipped into the anchors and set the ropes up for Gene, while Half Dome sat there in the shade, trickling waterfalls loomed in the distance, and birds circled us.

When Gene reached my point of the pendulum, he would have to do a lower-out, as I did on El Cap. I walked him through it, trying to remember how it went. He looked exactly how I felt two days ago, fumbling with the ropes, convincing himself that he was doing the right thing.

"Are you sure this is how it goes?" he said.

"I think so, yes. I mean, it is."

He finally figured it out, and we rappelled down to the ledge, leaving the rope fixed so that we could jumar up it in the morning.

We got comfortable on our bivy ledge, and it was one of the most glorious evenings of my life. I'd stayed at this ledge once previously on a failed attempt of the route, and that night I never quite felt calm or at ease. For whatever reason, this night was different. We stared at Half Dome as it finally got some of the days last rays of sun: gray granite with black water streaks and hints of orange. I had the feeling I was exactly where I was supposed to be. Gene and I were proud, and we were on the heels of success. All we had above us was climbing, and we didn't have to worry about the pains of hauling.

The simple Indian food out of a Tasty Bite package seemed like the best meal of my life. The one and a half beers we had were savored in small sips. (We lost half of one beer as the can had punctured, slowly leaking out into the haul bag.) We had two small speakers and a tiny iPod, and the music gently serenaded us with the high vibes and spirits of the vertical world.

I thought of the past, I thought of the climber who was killed on this very same ledge, by rockfall dislodged from another party high up on the route, on pitches not recommended to do by the guide because another party is almost always below you on this route. I thought of his partner, and his family, and how the incident affected them. Across from us on the two-thousand-plus-foot granite slab named Glacier Point, a young climber named Peter Terbush, from Gunnison, had been killed by rockfall in that crazy year of 1999. So much reminder of death, yet we felt safe, peaceful, content, alive, so psyched. I wondered what happened to their spirits, where they existed now?

I thought of my last bivy, unplanned and without sleeping gear, on the Painted Wall, in the Black Canyon, a sleepless night huddled next to my companion, shivering, just waiting for the endless night to be over. Perhaps that was why this bivy felt so good, so right, remembering the one that was full of dread and cold.

I thought of Layton Kor, the prolific climber of the 1960s who had established this route, as well as the Black Canyon route I suffered on in the unplanned bivy. I read in the guidebook that he and his partner, Chris Fredericks, didn't get to stay on this ledge but rather pressed on for higher terrain, eventually spending a sleepless night hanging in slings. I thought about how drive and passion for climbing can sometimes make one overlook the gentler, simpler fruits of life.

Most of all, I thought about how lucky I was to be up there with Gene. We were in sync and comfortable with one another in the vertical. He wanted this as badly as I did, and we were getting along famously. The boys came down and partied with us, as they promised. They were high on the vertical world too, and we made obscene jokes as guys do without women around and laughed as if we were old friends. Finally, it was time to sleep, and we drifted off with the cosmos. I was warm in my sleeping bag and could only fall asleep after I tied in with the rope, as Gene slept unroped on the huge ledge.

We woke up with the rays of the sun, forced down oatmeal and coffee, and pooped as one poops on a wall, first into a plastic bag, then stuffing the bag into the three-foot-long PVC pipe, called a poop tube. Immediately, Gene started jumaring up the rope we'd fixed the previous afternoon, and I followed right up after him. Finally, I had a flow to my jumar techniques and really felt good about how efficiently I was moving. We wanted to move quickly that day, both because success would be a big boost for our spirits and because we wanted our new friends to be successful as well.

As Gene started leading up a small, thin crack, we heard voices below, and it was Scott, with one of his friends, climbing up to the Thanksgiving Ledge. They were planning on a day climb of Southern Man, a harder route within spitting distance of ours. It was incredible to watch their pace as I split my time keeping an eye on Gene as he led and peering down as they raced up the wall. Gene fiddled above with nuts and cams, sliding them into the crack, as Scott did the same. They quickly reached our level, close enough that we could talk, and I picked Scott's brain about aid-climbing questions, and we made obscene jokes and shouted loudly and just generally hooted and hollered, buzzed on life in the vertical.

Clouds began forming, some grayness looming in the background, but no thunder or lightning. We had a good chance to get up this wall.

Scott's big wall climbing technique and demeanor is unique. He was talking to himself, singing a version of some reggae song and yelling at his partner the whole time, inching tiny stoppers and cam hooks in the cracks. "Oh God, this is sketchy," he said, all while having a smile on his face. A master at work.

Gene kept leading as I followed and cleaned. Our new friends below were progressing nicely, and all was well on the wall. Once they reached the belay where I was, it would usually be time for me to set off and clean the pitch. Finally, we finished the aid-climbing section, and it was time for a few pitches of free climbing, our element. We ditched a bag with the aid-climbing equipment at a belay, and I set off leading. The clouds were getting worse, and the wind was picking up. I tried to climb as fast as possible, while trying not to climb too fast and make a silly mistake, like a fall, that would slow us down. As I climbed, I felt so determined to get up the thing; this climb would define our trip.

At the second to last pitch, there was a point where there was an intimidating off-width-squeeze chimney above, the one Layton Kor had surely led on the first ascent. To the right was another option, an ugly, awkward seam that had been hammered with pitons. In our home multipitch area, the Black Canyon, that would have been unacceptable, to hammer an easier option just fifteen feet over from the true, proud line. But, every area has its own practices, and I opted for the quicker mode of climbing, the easier, quicker seam. I did make a mental note to return to take the prouder line. A great thing about climbing—those rocks will always be there.

Gene led the last pitch, with a funky, fun move over a small roof, and I followed up. We'd climbed the route. We shook hands, and it was anticlimactic, of course. Clouds and winds increased, and we knew we just had to get off this damn thing, so we rigged a rappel. The wind blew our ropes all over the place, and rappelling was a mixture of prayers and experience, just hoping the ropes would not get stuck, which could cause all types of problems.

We rappelled past Ben as he was leading up. He was struggling in a chimney section, and I remembered how he said the night before that he hated chimneys. I kept rappelling and noticed an anchor just to the right of where Patrick was belaying from, but didn't give much of a thought to its purpose and clipped into the bolts at Patrick's belay. Gene did the same, and we pulled the rope, hoping not to hit Ben. It was a bit of a clusterfuck.

As we pulled the rope, it got stuck, so we tugged some more, and, indeed, it was not going anywhere. We frantically yelled to Ben, "Can you see where it's stuck."

"Let me see what I can do," Ben said. "Oh shit, I can't move."

Our rope had wrapped around him and his gear, and he could not climb up. He had to rappel down. We felt so bad. Patrick had finally lost most of his patience with us but was still polite. What a guy! They wanted redemption and success on this wall, just as we did. Ben finally fixed everything, and, as he did so, I realized the adjacent set of anchors were for rappelling and set where they were so that the rope would not get stuck in the chimney above. Another lesson learned but at the expense of our new friends, damn. I wondered if we would have had the same patience with them if the roles had been reversed.

We kept rappelling, and the winds kept getting more and more intense as we came down. When we tossed the ropes, they went completely sideways, horizontal, and we just prayed they would not get stuck. Luckily they didn't. We finally reached the Dinner Ledge, gathering up our gear, and quickly headed down three more rappels, finally reaching the ground. Success! But, I couldn't help but feel bad as we looked up at the wall as Ben and Patrick were rappelling down. We could see their headlamps. Not only did they not reach the top, but also they had to rappel in the wind, in the dark.

We made it back to the Freedom Mobile, never hard to find in a parking lot, especially one with nice, shiny cars. We beelined it straight to the grocery store and bought beers to celebrate, meeting Scott back at the Green House for a humble dinner of pasta.

It stormed that night, and I slept in my tent to the sound of rain. Higher up, it had snowed. As we were making breakfast, we heard a knock on the door. It was a Scottish couple. They'd had an epic journey the night before, trying to drive into the Valley. They were following the GPS from their rental vehicle that had led them down a seldom-used 4x4 road. By the time they realized they needed to turn around, they were well down the road, and then they got stuck and had to spend the night sleeping in the vehicle. I wasn't surprised. In Foresta, it seems at least a car a day ends up in the area—the GPS programming is routed wrong for the region. We were happy to help and warmed them up with eggs and coffee, and we sat by the fireplace.

Eventually, we drove them into the Valley in the Freedom Mobile, dropping them off at the mechanic. I'd anticipated possibly needing the help of others during this trip, so we were more than happy to lend a helping hand, building up karma points in case we needed help at some point. This was not the first time we'd helped others on the trip: we'd already jumped two vehicles with the jumper cables Gene had wisely thrown in the back. For some reason, people knew they could reach out to the Freedom Mobile for help.

The rest of our time in Yosemite was a wash. It just kept raining and snowing, a sign to move on. Plus, time was winding down—I had to start my new house-sitting gig in my new town.

We spent a couple days chillin' at the Green House, drinking beer like we would be forever young. It did clear up the day we were leaving, and we were able to get a couple last pitches at the Cookie Cliff, some of the best shorter crack climbs in Yosemite.

I lead the last pitch for Yosemite: it was a nice finger-and-hand crack in a dihedral that made me want to linger and climb more. But, we had to go. Our spirits were high after that pitch, and we hopped in Freedom to leave Yosemite, grateful for our experiences and hungry for more.

Somehow, someway, we made it back to Colorado. I crashed with Gene in Telluride and then made the two-hour drive to Durango. Upon arrival at my new house, the woman who owned the place said it looked like the Freedom Mobile had been through a war. She was a sweet retired librarian, and she took care of her husband, who had aged faster than she had, and he was showing early signs of Alzheimer's. He was sweet too, but sad—I can only imagine what it's like to lose your memory. They were my saviors. I not only had a place to stay, but this was like a palace. Two bedrooms, a solarium, a garage, an entertainment room, and a nice spacious living room—a peaceful place to figure out my life. I'd successfully escaped the office life, but, the weirdest thing was, I wanted back in.

I hit the ground running in Durango. I was no longer wired to be lazy; I wanted to get a job like I had back at the college in Gunny. Naturally, I set up meetings at the college there, which was similar to Western, a small liberal arts school with just a few thousand students. I met with the president. She was brand new. They were faced with the same budget cutbacks Western was. There was simply nothing available. I pounded the pavement in town and looked for jobs. It was rough; I just couldn't find anything. I interviewed for smaller writing jobs but couldn't get anything. I had a small little nest egg for retirement from my last three years. All of a sudden, I was like a retired thirty-two-year-old, living in this plush middle-class home just outside of town.

Chapter 31

There were many things to worry about, but I was fortunate. I had a tiny bit of money, and I had a roof over my head. The economy would come back, right? I'd find a job, eventually. I wasn't proud; I'd go back to washing dishes if I had to, and, like always, I turned to nature and climbing for salvation.

It was the desert, again, like so many years before, that gave me hope and meaning. Durango was a perfect juxtaposition of mountains and desert. To the north and east were endless mountains and wilderness; you could be in the largest wilderness area in Colorado in fact, the

Weminuche, in less than an hour from leaving town.

It was that Colorado plateau desert though that captured me again. Now, the fight for my soul was a fight for purpose. I could handle being broke and unemployed. I'd been there before, but, losing my drive and purpose, that would be the death of my soul.

Fortunately, I did not fight the good fight alone. Tim had moved to Durango at exactly the same time. He'd left a job and moved there to start a new relationship. He was also fighting the demons of alcoholism, which had plagued him for some time.

Then, just like the old days, Two Tent Timmy rolled through town, and, of course, we rolled out to the desert.

This was the first of my winter experiences in Indian Creek. The snow that had settled on the ridges and buttresses painted a picture of a different place, a place before the tribe of modern climbers had claimed this land as a major destination on the circuit. Essentially, we had it all to ourselves. Occasionally, in the winter, you'll run into a party or two from Moab, Durango, or Telluride, but, more or less, it's just you and the ranchers out there, and the lizards, bunnies, and birds.

There's always an intoxication at Indian Creek; the feeling just changes from season to season. The nights would be cold, frigid, so we huddled around a fire or were content and sheltered in a sleeping bag. The nights were long and the stars were stark—this whole sky would give you something to see if you could get out of town.

The days are the best. When the sun is out, and the wind is absent, the rock is guaranteed to be warm enough, like a little forgotten secret that nature is constantly whispering. It was these moments, at the crag, which would stir my imagination. We all needed this freedom, this feeling. Tim was unemployed like me and working hard to quit drinking. Two Tent was on a break from work and had rambled back to Colorado. In its simplicity, the desert gave us the answers we needed.

What was going on in my friends' minds I'll never truly know, but I was wondering if I'd ever be able to get back that enthusiasm and momentum I just had, and lost. Would I be able to continue my career as a writer? I knew that was the only thing I'd be able to do for a living; the restaurant business was work, but it was not a career— washing dishes enables you to live hand to mouth, but it's not enough to support a family. And when would I find a woman like Lynn again? My heart was so drawn to Durango and to the desert. I had enough confidence in my decision, but there was always a lingering doubt. Did my own selfishness lead me down the wrong road? Looking out at the vast desert at high noon, with my two best friends, intoxicated by sunshine and the simple brotherhood of the rope, I thought for damn sure I was on the right path.

Two Tent stayed for about a month, and we got into a groove of heading out to Indian Creek for two or three days, then coming back to the Dirtbag Mansion, the name we'd given the house, and going back out to the Creek.

In no uncertain terms, my soul was saved by the desert, but, as I learned before, many times over, in the modern world, a man must continually fight for his place in the world. My way of fighting was writing.

I made a little place in the living room to write. I laid down two yoga blankets and sat on them for as long as I could while I wrote at this little table. It was like my solo pilgrimage—the pieces had finally come together to do my own thing with writing. And how odd was it that it took being jobless in the downturn of an economy to find my sweet spot with the thing I wanted to do for a living more than anything?

Of course, like everything, the time was limited. I was making a bad financial decision, liquidating my retirement funds before I was anywhere near the age of retiring, but I found peace of mind. I also thought of all the other people who were left unemployed by this recession, and I felt fortunate that I had still had passion. I also felt fortunate that I didn't have a mortgage to pay, or a family to support. My dreams were still in my grasp. What more could a man ask for in such a precarious position?

It took months to actually get my first story with the paper going. I wasn't a local and therefore didn't know what was going on around town, so I had no story ideas. All the writing I was doing was unpaid, just tales I wanted to tell from the last few years that I didn't have time for before when I was working in the office full time. One day in the throes of winter, I came across an event in Ouray, the ice climbing Mecca of Colorado, just two hours north, called "Gimps On Ice," put on by Paradox Sports.

It was a totally politically incorrect name for such a festival, a climbing event where disabled climbers gathered to celebrate unity and climbing on ice. I'd quit ice climbing years ago, but when the *Telegraph* said I could write the article, I figured I had to come out of retirement.

Several years earlier, I'd become acquainted with Paradox by a random encounter in Indian Creek. We were out there to celebrate Creeksgiving, the holiday we created at Thanksgiving—basically a bunch of dirtbags eating well, dressing up in costumes, and having dance parties, and this particular year it was raining like crazy. When it rains in the desert, climbing just doesn't happen, so those of us that had our bikes on the tops of our cars went for a little tour to get some exercise. Halfway up Beef Basin Road, we saw this car driving back and forth. It had Texas plates with a handicapped tag hanging off the rearview mirror. We were sure this person was not a climber and was wildly lost. The car slowed down, and the guy got out. We watched him step out of the car, and the guy was missing a leg. He set his artificial leg onto the dirt and asked for a lighter. He lit up a cigarette and told us he was looking for his friend, but he couldn't seem to find him.

His name was Chad, and he was a veteran. His leg had been blow off by a bomb in Iraq. He had the look of a hippie with a long-gone stare of a veteran of war. Years ago, when 9/11 happened, I was full of anger when we went to war, but I never had to go to war. Chad did. I listened to his every word. He risked his life and gave his leg for the war. I simply raised my voice in college. His actions spoke louder.

That night he told us stories about war and Paradox Sports, and also engaged in some friendly wrestling in the dirt. Just like that, we had a new friend in the crew.

At the "Gimps" event—the name was later tamed down to something more politically correct—everyone had a story. It was a goldmine for a writer like me, desperate not only to tell my own stories but those of other people. Mine could only be told with the grace of prose and poetry; these people were walking, talking, living, breathing miracles. One Arm Pete was one of the first guys I met. He was a former Durango guy. I'd read an article about him in *Climbing* magazine by John Sherman in 2000, back in those pre-Internet climbing-website days when I read and memorized every photo and line in the mags. He was born with a right arm that was only developed to his elbow and was a better climber than many with two fully formed arms.

Then there was Stacy. He was a giant of a guy, who probably seemed intimidating until he spoke a single word, and then everything changed. You could just tell he was a troubled, but lovable teddy bear. I'd started a climbing zine and showed Stacy a copy when we met. The first sentence in the first climbing zine I ever put together was, "Without climbing, I'd be dead or in jail." Stacy read that line and a tingle went down his spine; he gave me a crazy look and told me the same thing was true for him.

Stacy was a vet too, but came back all intact. Just because you don't lose a limb at war doesn't mean you come back the same. Stacy was deeply affected by PTSD and became addicted to drugs and alcohol after he returned from Iraq and Afghanistan, which turned him into a suicidal mess, a living casualty of war. A climb in the Flatirons of Boulder saved his life, gave him something to live for. It was the first and only time a deep bond was cemented in my life by a single sentence. We were buddies forever, right then and there, and it was a validation in this risk, this leap I was taking in my life.

Everyone at Gimps On Ice had these crazy stories, and, though it might seem counterintuitive, ice climbing is the perfect sport for someone who is missing a limb. Everyone already uses ice tools for their hands and crampons for their feet. When I watched guys like One Arm Pete climb ice, it didn't seem like anything was missing. He flowed smoothly up the vertical ice, one swing of the ice tool at a time.

From this whole crew, I made some lifelong friends in a weekend, wrote my first story for my new newspaper gig, and gained that ever-important thing called perspective. Though I was struggling and was going to struggle more, there were many things in life to remain positive about. And, climbing was the key to unlocking it all.

After months of ferocious writing, climbing, getting to know my new town, and extreme relaxing comparative to retirement, spring was over, and the owners returned to their house. Two Tent came back for another visit and helped me clean the place from top to bottom. The owners were pleased. I'd done my job, and I started to lay a foundation in this town that very much suited me. But I still didn't have a steady job, and I started to have dreams of Yosemite again. And what does a climber dreaming of climbing do when he does not have a job?

Two Tent and I teamed up with Shaun and met him in Gunnison. Shaun and I had planned a trip together one summer a few years back, but had an argument about something stupid and didn't do the trip together. We fought like brothers, but also had brotherly love.

We stashed the Freedom Mobile at a friend's house, packed up Shaun and Two Tent's vehicles and rallied out to Yosemite. It had been years since I'd been there with Two Tent.

There were signs from the beginning. Omens. The first was the weed-smoking incident that probably saved our lives. We were in the thick of it in Nevada, headed west on Highway 50, the loneliest highway in America, the ocean of desert that separates Colorado from California.

We stopped along the roadside, at an incognito place, to smoke a bowl. Some say marijuana impairs driving, but, in the heart of the desert, I'd argue that it helps. Break the monotony. Make the clouds look more interesting and the music sound more soothing. Embrace the road. So I smoked some herb, and we did some push-ups to balance it out, and then we were back on the road.

Three miles in, there was a woman on the side of the road waving her hands frantically. And then we saw why: an eighteen-wheeler flipped over perfectly sideways in the oncoming lane. The scene had an aura of death. Was the driver alive? It didn't look like it. And, wait, what if, what if we had not stopped? Was there a higher power at hand, or were we just lucky? Climbers need luck, sometimes as much they need skill. And, we're all facing that semi that is death; we just hope to dodge it day after day. We drove slowly by passing the semi, which incredibly didn't block off the road, only the other lane.

It was the perfect trio to balance out personalities. Two Tent Timmy, and my brother from another mother, Shaun. Two Tent is the nicest guy in the world, soft spoken and easy going. Shaun is incredibly driven, believes he can do anything, and he's an aid-climbing master. I'm driven and often selfish, but climbing keeps me in check. When I climb with someone often that means I love them, and what I love about climbing is the necessary teamwork. Nothing can be accomplished alone. It forces me to elevate, to grow.

We slept off the side of the road in the Nevada desert that night. The type of sleep you have when you're far away from home, and you're surrounded by the odd desert in an unfamiliar place. We steered through Nevada into California but made all the wrong turns. Relieved to be in California, we slept in a parking lot and awoke early before we were noticed. Way too late, we rolled into Yosemite.

Yosemite Valley stopped me dead in my tracks the first time, but now everything is just a ritual. El Capitan is still there, and it still causes tourists to lose their minds. They just halt the cars, stand in the road, and stare. Tourists are stupid. And maybe we are as well. We had driven a thousand miles to toil on faces of stone.

The ritual. Arrive, meet up with friends, do some cragging, pick an objective, and then begin the ritual of all rituals: packing the haul bag.

We set up at Scott's house in Foresta. His time had run out at the Green House, and he was now living just up the block with his girlfriend.

The tarp. Everything was laid out on the tarp, and the absurdity of aid climbing started to settle in. So much gear, so much water—why were we doing this again? Smoked weed. Spaced out. Focused on the task at hand. Forgetting one small piece of gear could derail the whole climb. Fit it all in the haul bag. It was always overflowing. Did we have the poop tube? Were we ready to move slowly up an overhanging wall? Was this going to be fun? Were we still psyched?

We humped all the gear to the base of the wall. The hike and the base of the wall were littered with trash and booty. But the booty was questionable—we found a couple of old pitons and biners—gear that was probably dropped years ago, and then the storms of spring washed them down into the gully.

We camped at the base of the wall, and, in the morning, we planned to start up. It's Two Tent's first aid climb. Shaun has climbed El Capitan. He's the only veteran of big wall climbing. Two Tent was new to it all. He'd never even used ascenders.

After the usual rituals of necessity—oatmeal, coffee, and pooping—we readied ourselves for the climb. A fourth-class traversing section must be negotiated, and immediately the struggle began. We clipped into a fixed rope as we moved the pig along. The pig, this beast of burden, was about to unleash its awkward and cruel nature upon us.

Instead of shuffling the haul bag along, Two Tent hoisted it on his back like a normal pack. Just minutes after doing this, while making a delicate move on a step across, he slipped. All of a sudden, he was turned upside down. Fuck, if he hadn't been clipped in to that fixed rope, he would have just fallen to his death. We pulled him upright and his look of terror and shock was something I've never seen in my years of climbing with him. His face was all scratched up and bleeding. A lesser man would have suggested retreat. But we carried on. And then it was time for him to learn how to jug.

A severely overhanging bolt ladder started the climb. When it's time for Two Tent to jumar up, he was sent into space. Shaun carefully lowered him out from the belay, and then, hanging in space, with five hundred feet of air below him, on one's of the world's steepest big walls, he learned.

I lead more straightforward terrain, and then, when the aid climbing became more difficult, Shaun took over. He loved the challenge of tricky aid. For me, it's a means to an end. Free climbing is my thing. And it was Two Tent's thing as well. We hung at an uncomfortable belay and listened to music. Willie Nelson singing sad country. We were in our own moment of despair. Two Tent was brought into this idea of aid climbing, when I'm sure all he wanted to do was go up free routes by day and gather around to eat, drink, and be merry by night. And who wouldn't want to do that? What was the point of all of this?

El Capitan was the point.

The pitch had some strange aid rating of C2F, and much of the fixed gear had been removed or had fallen out. Shaun meticulously worked through everything. I had concerns about him on this trip. He was coming off a sickness that he concluded was either rocky mountain tick fever or dengue from a recent trip to Thailand. Either way, his body was not at 100 percent, but his mind was running at full speed, and he had a strong desire for success on Yosemite's big walls.

It was one of those belays that seemed like an eternity, and I questioned our sanity and the expected outcome of this experience in my mind. The silence was defeating and puzzling. I was willing to suffer, but I think Two Tent was wondering why the hell he'd gotten on board with this plan. Eventually, Shaun completed the pitch, and, when I jugged up, I was impressed by his creativity with nuts, hooks, and small cams.

By late afternoon, we'd arrived at the Ahwahnee Ledge, and we were done with hauling for the day. Time to set ourselves up for success the following day. I led another pitch and took a twenty-footer when a nut popped. Shaun was on his way to drifting asleep when I fell, and the tension on his gri-gri snapped him back to reality. The fall energized us both. A fall can be liberating, and this one certainly was. I pulled up on the rope and completed the pitch.

That night was quiet and defeating. It was Two Tent's first. I typically either feel exhaustedly comfortable or full of dread while sleeping on a wall. This time it was the latter. While it was comfortable, the vibes were wearing on me. I awoke in the middle of the night to a light rain, and babbled to my companions about starting to climb. Delusion. The rain didn't last, and we woke up in the morning and drank coffee, ate oatmeal, and pooped.

A haze of fog surrounded us, giving the illusion that we were about to be socked in a storm. More dread. More fear, more of a sense that we were fighting against the Gods of the walls and karma. After jugging up to our high point, we were totally immersed in the fog. Should we bail? "If you go down, you can always go back up," a big wall climber once told me. That voice rang true, and we decided to bail.

Bailing on an overhanging wall while carrying a haul bag was something I'd never done. Shaun quickly figured out a system, and the first person down clipped themselves into directionals so they could reach the belay. At one point, I spent five minutes trying to swing in to a bolted belay. Dangling above the foggy, mysterious void, I felt frustration and a slight hatred for this form of climbing. When it's good, it's good, but when it's purely a struggle, more than any other discipline of climbing, it makes me wonder why. Why should I do this?

When we arrived back to the horizontal, the sky opened up to blue. We could have continued to the top and started our trip with success. But, instead, it's midday and time for ice cream and beer. Tourists asked us questions and took our photos. "Isn't it scary up there?" they asked. No worse than down here in this strange horizontal world, I think. "Yeah, it can be scary," I said. It can. I have mixed feelings about wall climbing.

The following week and a half was stormy and cold. With bad weather—Why do we always say *bad*? It's just bad for climbing, but it's good for life!—we turned into tourists ourselves. Cloudy, rainy, and snowy days changed our routine into survival. Days were spent at the Curry Village Lodge, huddled up to do Internet work. There were others like us, from all sorts of countries that fester. Yosemite is not the best place for festering. It's not the worst either—amenities galore, and there's time and places to write.

I got a phone call from my friend Jon, who has just had a climbing accident in the Black Canyon. He fell when a ledge collapsed on him while he was trying to reach a rappel. After time in the hospital, his worst injury was a broken nose. He's in good spirits. Like a punch-drunk boxer, he will return to climbing hard routes in the Black.

One night, I talked to my parents on the phone and gave them an update on our trip. My parents always show unconditional love, and, through this episode of vagabonding and unemployment, they were still supportive. During this phone call, they have sad news: my brother's good friend from childhood succumbed to brain cancer. He's gone, and his wife was about to deliver their first baby. It snowed around me, and gloomy, snowy weather fit the news. What can you really say about a young man dying?

Finally we got tired of the gloom and went to the beach. Some people dream of vacations at the beach; for us it was a distraction. We secured a small cottage to stay at on a couch-surfing website. The people were super hippies, real California hippies, and they basically handed us the keys to their house upon arrival. There was a rabbit, and we fed him lettuce. How did they know they could trust us? I guess there wasn't much to steal; books seemed to be their most valuable possession. I think the world would be a better place if more people's most valuable possessions were books.

When we returned to the Valley, there was a good weather window, so we set our hearts on El Capitan. We chose Lurking Fear, one of the more moderate routes on The Captain. Again, we laid out the tarp and packed up.

After a week and a half of storms, El Cap was drying out. Two Tent left, back to Oregon for work, and I stayed with Shaun, who finally seemed to be back to 100 percent. If things went perfectly, we could climb El Cap and then head back home. Plus, there was a carrot dangling at the top of the wall—his girlfriend had a timeshare trade with someone in Las Vegas, and we could stay there for a few days on our way back to Colorado. There was a lazy river and everything—we could live like dirtbag ballers.

El Capitan stood as proudly as ever, with long streaks of water running down its side in the shade. In the sun, everything was drying out. An ocean of granite, and we were about to set sail.

Our first day was full of slow progress. We brought a portaledge, and hauling, like always, was a pain. Shaun led for the day, and I sunk into cleaning, and staring, lots of staring. It was nice to be on El Cap.

We set up the portaledge. Well, rather we fought with the portaledge and constantly adjusted it. Finally, it was secure and mostly even. It was blissful, and we drank a beer that we'd stashed in the haul bag. We achieved a level of happiness that we'd been seeking for the last two weeks. Shaun loved the mechanics of aid climbing, and I was grateful to be up there with him.

The next morning, we broke down the portaledge. It was my lead. I set off with a gigantic rack. The pitch started with a section you could either aid with hooks or free climb at 5.10. I tried to free climb, but the massive rack weighed me down. I must have gone up and down ten times. Defeated, I climbed back to the belay and sat there in frustration. If I was a better aid climber, I would have committed to using hooks, but the free climber in me was convinced I could complete the section. After sitting at the belay for an hour and contemplating, I went up without the rack, climbed through the section, and, once I was at a ledge higher up, I hauled up the rack. A revelation: float like a butterfly.

Our progress was painfully slow, but we had the route to ourselves. We only managed a few pitches that day. Failure was in the air. Our movement was snail like, and we did not have enough food to be up there for the pace at which we were moving. On the last pitch Shaun cleaned, he left several nuts in the crack that were difficult to remove. It was implied we would bail the next day.

The portaledge was less glorious than the night before. After all, this was the final day in the vertical on a trip full of failures. I'd been climbing long enough to know that every success is built upon failure. Plus, Shaun and I were getting along and working together, and that alone was a success.

In the morning, I woke up uncomfortable. And I had morning wood. I can say that, in my days of climbing, there is nothing that can compare to the dismal letdown of waking up next to another man on a portaledge when you have morning wood. Of course, I didn't say a word about my condition, and it quickly went away once I recognized where I was. We started water for coffee and oatmeal.

Suddenly, we noticed a party behind us. And they were moving fast. Quickly they arrived at our perch. What took us two days to climb and haul, they'd just completed as we took our first sips of coffee. Bastards. The leader had removed some of the nuts we'd left in the crack below that we'd planned to retrieve when we bailed. They were full of energy, and we were full of defeat. There was an argument between the leader and us; he was trying to booty our nuts. "I didn't realize you were free climbing," he said, thinking the only reason to leave gear in the crack below was that we were working it for a free climbing attempt.

We didn't explain ourselves very well, but we got most of our gear back from him. This guy was going for El Cap In a Day, and he was preoccupied with getting a couple small pieces of free gear. Only a climber would be such a dirtbag.

Luckily his buddy was much friendlier. He told us it was cool how we were climbing El Cap in the style we were. I thought exactly the opposite. They had nothing but one rope and a rack of gear, going for it, climbing the wall in a day. Proud. His forearms oozed pure strength. He said he'd never used a haul bag or a ledge; he just did everything in a day. He wasn't a famous climber we'd ever heard of, just another low-key badass flying under the radar. We liked him, and I hoped to climb like him someday. Instead, we would bail with a still very heavy haul bag and portaledge.

We spent our day figuring out the logistics of bailing with the heavy loads. We did the walk of shame along the base of El Cap and tried not to make eye contact, so we wouldn't have to explain our predicament. Then we had a beer and stared at El Cap from the meadow. And then we had ice cream and stared at Half Dome from another meadow. The next day we left for Las Vegas and then went back home to Colorado.

Chapter 32

I'm dying for some action
I'm sick of sitting 'round here trying to write this book

—*Bruce Springsteen, "Dancing In The Dark"*

I escaped to Crested Butte for the rest of the summer and lived in a small trailer with my buddy Shane. I partied too much and wrote too little. I washed some dishes but, other than that, didn't really work. I was lost and floating. When a friend of a friend offered me a gig trimming marijuana in Southern Oregon, I couldn't pass it up. I was hard up for money and, at this point, had no pride.

Twelve of us sat at a picnic table and plucked buds of weed from their plants, all day every day. There was an air of paranoia because the feds were in town doing flyovers in planes, checking to see if the operations were above the legal limit. The owner of the property was a drunk and drank all day every day. We were offered as much beer as we wanted, and I tried to hold out as long as I could. I waited until everyone else had one, and then I started drinking. Day after day of sitting and drinking—all romantic notions I'd given to the life of weed trimming dissipated. After the two weeks that seemed like two months, we were released from the property. Two weeks without exercise and I felt like hell.

I wandered Oregon some after that because we'd expected to work longer than two weeks, but all I wanted then was to get back to Colorado. I felt so lost. After a few days of climbing at Smith Rocks, I changed my plane ticket and arrived back home. Tim was there at the airport to pick me up, and I couch surfed at his place until my house-sitting gig started.

I moved into yet another nice middle-class house for a few months. The owners were horse people and said there was a neighbor who had a bunch of horses and needed some help. They said she would pay cash, so naturally I inquired.

This job was the shit. Rather, it involved shit. The lady, who was sweet and had a brother who was a climber that died young, needed help with mucking the areas where the horses hung out. At this point, a year into being unemployed, I no longer had pride. I mucked the horseshit.

Again, I got into a routine of writing. Damn, if that was the only thing that saved me. I was still climbing, but I knew then and forever that climbing was only an ingredient and a constant—it would never save me. I couldn't make money from climbing, I couldn't make love to it, and it could not feed me.

Eventually, the owners of the house came back, like they always do, and, for the first time, I rented a place in town. I'd always lived on the outskirts of Durango and never fully immersed myself in the city limits. I rented a room from a couple I'd become friends with. The house was right next to the library. In all these wandering years, a library was home just as much as any place I was renting for the short term.

Winter's blanket covered Durango, and our sleepy place was a nice little home, and it was comforting to live with friends instead of all alone in a big place. I could just hop on a bike and head over to yoga or the coffeeshop to read a book.

On a sunny January morning, I got that phone call you absolutely never want to get: Adam had died in an avalanche. Tim was ice climbing in Ouray when he got the news, and he'd left me a message in the middle of the night that I didn't get until that morning. It was the end of innocence for our friends. I'd never lost a close friend from my old Gunny crew before.

Everyone handles death differently, but I learned then, forever, that the closer you are to that person, and the more you depend on them day to day, the deeper it cuts. I wasn't as close to Adam as some of my other friends, like Shaun and Tim. I had to call several friends and break the news to them. Immediately, I felt Adam's spirit with me. He was watching over me, just as he had when I needed a couch to crash on in my dark days in Salt Lake City. The dream was not over, but he had departed from his body and would only be a part of my dreams in the spiritual form now.

I cried and cried and wrote out a little something for Adam that I sent to the local papers back in the Gunnison Valley. I wished I could have known him more. He believed in me and my writing at a time when I did not, in those dark days. He was my light, and, through feeling his presence after his death, I knew he would continue to be a light.

Shaun and I ended up in Salt Lake City the week after Adam died for the Outdoor Retailer trade show. The very day Adam died in the avalanche, I'd left him a message to see if we could crash at his house while we were there. Of course, he would have said yes. He would have been proud too; we were up there on business to promote my writing and make connections. We still stayed at his house.

He was the first of us to buy his own house. There was an aura of sadness, with his girlfriend and roommate both grieving just as we were. All throughout his house were his simple possessions—his bookshelf of paperbacks and guidebooks, his bikes, skis, boating gear, and climbing gear. A lone houseplant—a flower was blooming.

Adam was one of the goofiest people I'd ever known, with a laugh that seemed to come up from his sides and go all the way to the crinkles in his face. Now, I don't know how this started, but he began carrying an obscure piece of climbing gear, a pink tri-cam, with him on every big outdoor excursion he would go on. It didn't matter if he would use it or not; even on a skiing trip, he would take it and snap a summit photo with it.

That last day in Salt Lake, all walking outside of Adam's house with our heads hung low, Shaun noticed something in the freshly fallen snow: the pink tri-cam. Somehow it had ended up, randomly, in the sidewalk, and we retrieved it. Shaun still has it to this day, tucked away in his room, a sentimental reminder of our friend that passed on to the next adventure.

In Durango, when spring rolled around, I was finishing up my very first book, a collection of short stories. My confidence seemed to change then, like I was no longer a literary virgin. I had that tangible proof that I was a writer, and my work would finally be sold in a bookstore.

I was also out of money. I'd liquidated my retirement funds and every other sort of resource that I had. It was time to get a job. I applied for gigs at the college again but didn't get hired. One day, I was eating at my favorite little burrito joint, where I ate lunch almost every day because it was cheap, and I started up a conversation with one of the managers. I asked if they needed a dishwasher, and he said no but they needed some other kitchen help, and, just like that, I finally had a job in Durango.

I hated it at first. Maybe it was my ego, or the fact that they started me in the kitchen, and almost everyone else was Mexican and spoke Spanish, and my Spanish sucks. When it comes down to it, I feel like I've let myself down with the Spanish language. I should know it by now. I studied it in school, I've traveled to Mexico many times, and yet I barely know enough to order beer and a taco.

It was madness in the kitchen that summer; the restaurant was one of the busiest in Durango, and I was learning their system. To top it off, I just wanted to wash dishes, and they were having me prep food. Plus, the dishwasher hated me for some reason. I thought that was quite the karmic coincidence, considering I'd paid my dues a thousand times over as a dish diver. One day, I was about to confront him when I learned some valuable information: the dishwasher had gone to jail for five years for stabbing someone. The owner, who was a nice and generous man, was giving him another chance at freedom. Once I learned he'd stabbed someone, I decided against a confrontation with him. Just a few months later he was back in jail anyways. Sad.

After paying my dues in the restaurant, in the kitchen, I was moved up to the front of the house. I'd always been a dishwasher, but it was nice to try something new. It was so humbling after my days in higher education—I was back to the grind, in a very blue-collar way. The owner and the managers all knew about my writing aspirations, and they thought it was super cool I was trying to make it on my own as a writer. When they needed a new manager, they asked me, and I promptly said no, even though it entitled me to a raise as well. A few months later, they asked me again. I told them I would do it if I could have as much time off to travel and climb as I wanted. They agreed.

So when I asked off for a week and a half to go back to Yosemite, no one even flinched. I was the only climber there, and they thought it was inspiring that I wanted to try to climb El Capitan. I bought a plane ticket, and, just like that, I was off again to the Mecca.

The trip started in Las Vegas. Dave was there, with his girlfriend Brittney, and was doing some climbing to prepare for a guiding exam later in the month. I had a knot in my stomach. I had to face my greatest fear, El Capitan, and there was no turning back.

So I was off to Las Vegas with my bags full of hope, and gear. The helmet was the only thing that wouldn't fit in the bags, so I put it in the overhead compartment. The flight was full of young and old, excited for Vegas and the simple sinning it provides. I'd been to Vegas, many times, and I no longer got excited to gamble and binge drink.

Then something happened. My helmet was dislodged from the overhead compartment and fell on an old lady's head. She was creepy and reminded me of one of those monsters from *Fear and Loathing in Las Vegas*. She freaked out and started yelling, "Whose bike helmet was that?"

Fortunately there was a bike trip on that flight, and she assumed it was one of theirs. I sat there and said nothing.

We climbed in the extreme heat of Vegas. It made me feel woozy and lightheaded. That night we stayed in Campganistan, the shitty BLM campsite outside of Red Rocks. The next morning, we drove through the desert to Yosemite.

Again, we stayed with Scott. That night I slept restlessly and awoke in fear. John Long once wrote that, "Anybody who says he slept well, or at all, before that first big climb, is either crazy or a liar." And he's right.

Our plan was to not waste any time and get right on Free Blast, the ten-pitch start to the Salathe Wall, our line of choice. We would nip hesitation in the bud and leave our rack and a rope up on the Heart Ledges, where we would haul to and bivy the following day.

We arrived at the start of the route at the same exact time as another party. They were as friendly as could be and attempting to free climb Free Rider, a route that shares many pitches with the Salathe. That day, everything went as planned, and leaving our stash of gear on the Heart Ledges was an act of commitment.

We spent a day hauling the pig up to the Heart Ledges, a relatively straightforward haul, and everything went fine. We arrived to find four cans of Pabst Blue Ribbon at the ledge, where we would spend the night. They looked unpleasant—aluminum cans of beer baking in the sun. When we arrived at that ledge, I had a feeling of being exactly where I wanted to be in my life. So much had been leading up to this moment, years of dreams and failures. The man who knows endurance can know success.

Dave and I basked at this ledge for a while, getting our sleeping situation arranged and hooting and hollering on life. Then we fixed a pitch and talked with some Austrian climbers who wanted to pass us. The leader had muscles that probably ripped all his shirts out, so he was wearing a tank top with the sides ripped. His companions seemed to have titles: the second and the photographer. He must have been some famous climber back home. The leader climbed with focus and ease while his buddies seemed to be on edge, especially the photographer. They inquired about the cans of PBR; immediately, we saw their future value, and we agreed to let them have two cans, and we would take the other two—democracy with foreigners.

On the ledge that night, I felt at home and at ease. We were on the rock of our dreams. And Dave was the perfect partner. He was better at figuring out the logistics of hauling and jugging. Dave was the ying to my yang. Plus, we'd struck a deal: I would lead the infamous Hollow Flake, and he would lead the notoriously wet Sewer pitch.

I slept well, but, once we began the climbing for the day, there was intense dread running through my entire being. It was Hollow

Flake. Supposedly it was a solid 5.9 off-width that didn't have much gear. One guy told me that, after leading it, he was unable to move for the rest of the day; he just collapsed at the belay and didn't have the desire to climb any higher. Others just looked at me as if I were about to go through a rite of passage, which I was.

The knot in my stomach grew tighter. Finally, after a couple straightforward pitches, it was the moment of truth. I climbed up to a pendulum, lowered out, and swung over the off-width. I fiddled with some gear to no avail. The crack was too wide. I called down to him at the belay, "Dave, can you send up that Big Bro?"

"We didn't bring the Big Bro," he yelled back.

So I sunk into the crack with a thousand feet of granite below me and performed the off-width techniques I'd learned over the years. I've always liked off-widths, in that masochistic, fucked-up kinda way, but most of my experience was at Indian Creek. Well-protected off-widths they were, where I could always hang on gear if needed. Here I was climbing higher and higher, above the void, with my last piece of protection in the void as well, a good thirty feet down and ten feet over to the right. If I were to fall, it would be a monster.

For the next seventy feet, I climbed through a lifetime of climbing fear with no gear other than a tipped out #6 Camalot. At one point, I thought I was facing the wrong way and did that ridiculous shuffle, switching sides in the middle of a pitch, which was like wrestling a wet alligator, and if you let go of him, your climbing career could be over then and there. I was terrified. Then I realized I had to get this thing done. The climb, the dream, could not be sustained if we were unsuccessful on this pitch. I'd never dug my arms so deep into an off-width, and I prayed to the gods of the vertical for passage. My heels and toes were equally pressed as firmly into the crack. After a while, I was completely in the moment, with my body and muscles giving their best efforts. When I finally arrived at that belay, an ocean of relief washed over me. Adrenaline covered every cell of my being. I whooped, "Off belay," to Dave and fixed the line for him.

There was more off-width that day, but it was better protected, so it is not as etched into my memory. Dave took a block of pitches that led us into the night, and we arrived just below the El Cap Spire to a nice ledge with plenty of sleeping room. The friendly guys attempting Free Rider were there and kindly offered us the best sleeping spots. They had a portaledge, and we had nice spots to sleep. It was a long and tiring day, and arriving to such a welcoming spot was much needed. We exchanged pleasantries, and we were equally excited for each other. Their attempt at free climbing was successful thus far, and we were more than halfway up The Captain. We didn't speak of the horizontal world below; no one resorted to the "So, what do you do?" question. We were just brothers of the vertical and shared food, drink, and smoke.

They were off early in the morning, and we sat around lazily and drank coffee. Now this is why I like Dave; he'll get business done when it's time, but he recognizes how equally important it is to sit and take stock of your surroundings. It's not every day the towering pine trees below seems like small bushes in the garden of life, and it's equally as rare for me to feel free and unchained on a big wall. We just barely had everything we needed. A small space to sit, a little water, some food, and coffee—that fueled the high of the morning. It didn't matter how much money was in our bank accounts, or what jobs we had, or where we came from, and where we were going. It was the reunion with the original spirit of rock climbing I loved so much. Plus, we recognized that this might be a one-time thing. Many climbers make countless trips up El Cap, but we knew this might be the only time we would ever be up there.

We climbed again after an extended hour of glorious coffee drinking. Straightforward pitches led to the dreaded Sewer pitch, described in the guidebook as the "worst pitch of the route." It was supposed to always be wet and seeping, and no one I'd ever talked to enjoyed the pitch. Some described shivering while leading it, and then waiting an eternity at the belay until the haul bag arrived with warm clothes. I was glad Dave was going to lead it.

Our good fortune continued when we arrived to find that the Sewer was bone dry. That luck didn't carry on to our bivy, when we ended up staying at the Block, a terribly sloping bivy, owned by the fire ants that kept biting us. Some ledges are made for sleeping, and some are made for just making it through the night. We laughed at the situation and had a restless night of sleep. The motivation that kept us positive: we would stand on top of El Capitan the next day.

Our free climbing friends passed us early in the morning and, of course, were overly polite. We were blessed with their company. When you're doing a trade route on El Cap in the prime season, you're bound to share the wall with others. And they can shape your experience. They were headed into 5.12 terrain at six in the morning as the sun was barely coming up. We drank coffee, ate oatmeal, and pooped.

When we gained higher terrain, we found that our friends were defeated. They had managed a free ascent to this point, twenty-some pitches up, but kept falling on one move in a dihedral. They decided to rappel back down, which, in my mind, was a crazy thought—all I wanted to do was go up. Down they went, with the air of failure. "I don't know if this is for me," one of the climbers said. I knew the feeling.

Then things started to get real steep. A traversing pitch under a roof brought us to the headwall. I got twisted around in the ropes with more than two thousand feet of air beneath me. I felt sick to my stomach. That's climbing for you—one moment it's ecstasy and you're on the mountain of your dreams, the next moment, you feel like you're going to vomit on the mountain of your dreams. Then I led the headwall, a perfect seam that took textbook cam placements.

We arrived at Long Ledge, a narrow ledge you could sleep on, with the massive void below. The exposure and steepness were mind blowing—one of those things you just have to experience, even if it's just once, in your lifetime. It was there, and then it was gone, but it's always there.

Off Long Ledge, there was one more challenging pitch: a runout above a small piece of gear. As I traversed out and started the pitch, I noticed a piece of fixed gear. Upon closer inspection, I saw that it was a pink tri-cam. I was awash in a spiritual feeling, like Adam was watching over us, and he was proud. I yelled up to the sky, to Adam. Climbing on a big wall will make you believe that random things like this are indeed signs.

I rested at a perch for a minute and took it all in. I realized I was perfectly at ease, comfortable, relaxed; all I had to do was dance from hold to hold. I switched out my approach shoes for climbing shoes and delicately moved up the wall. Seldom in my life have I felt that calm on a runout, and I'd surely never been that exposed.

A couple more straightforward pitches led us to the top. For me, summits are usually anticlimactic. This one was different. The sky around us started to fade into an intense orange-and-red display of wonder. With the difficulty over, as I stood on that summit, I yelled and whooped for joy. I thought of everyone that was close to me and said a prayer of gratitude. It was the greatest climb of my life, and yet in the climbing world, it was so simple, so routine.

When Dave found a couple extra packages of tuna I was convinced we'd already eaten, we danced and screamed. I don't even like tuna. But when you take things away and enter the vertical world, a new appreciation is gained for the simple things in life. I knew that was part of the reason I'd stuck with this climbing thing, and all my years of toil and suffering had paid off. This was as much a moment of clarity as it was a climbing accomplishment.

Then the magic wore off. We had a restless night sleeping on the summit. We awoke and had just enough water to either make coffee or oatmeal. We went with coffee. On the final descent, we had the most dangerous moment of the adventure: Dave started to lose his balance on a fourth-class slab while carrying the haul bag, which was still surprisingly heavy considering we'd eaten all the food and drank all the water. He made some terrifying noises, and I'd never seen him so spooked. Fortunately, he kept it together and didn't fall.

When we arrived back to Scott's, the magic had returned. We ate a pound of bacon and drank a beer. We pretty much ate everything we saw for the next couple days. It was the time of the annual Yosemite Facelift cleanup, and we partied with the climbing community that night.

The next day, we learned about "wall hands" when our hands swelled up from days of jamming and other abuse. Eventually, we made our way to the El Cap Meadow. It was surreal and a confirmation that sometimes it's more difficult to look at The Captain and wonder if it's possible for you than it is to actually climb it.

Chapter 33

Our high lasted for days. Dave and I were drunk on our success and camaraderie. Even when we arrived back in Las Vegas, we still had that crazy, awesome feeling. In the grand scheme of things, we'd achieved nothing. The standards in the climbing world are so high, the athleticism so intense, that a climb like the one we did is quite routine. We did it for all the right reasons though, and it was hard, for us. That's what matters in climbing—the style, the motivation, the friendship and camaraderie, and, above all, the feeling, the place it brings you, internally and externally.

This was years ago, and I wish I could say that I've climbed El Capitan many times since then, but the truth is I haven't even touched it in those years that have passed. It is a perfect memory, and I haven't purposely avoided climbing on El Cap to protect a memory—that's just the way life has gone. I've spent much more time in the mellow Colorado Plateau desert, finding the unclimbed lines, basking in the transcendence that place has to offer, realizing the Golden Age of American climbing is not over, and maybe, there, it has just begun.

Chapter 34

This is the most beautiful place on earth. There are many such places. Every man, every woman, carries in the heart and mind the image of the ideal place, the right place, the one true home, known or unknown, actual or visionary...

For myself, I'll take Moab, Utah. I don't mean the town itself, of course, but the country which surrounds it—the canyonlands. The slickrock desert. The red dust and the burnt cliffs and the lonely sky—all that which lies beyond the end of the roads.

Desert Solitaire by Edward Abbey

So there, in the desert, came a parting image for my climbing career in my thirties, which, building on the base of experience and the reality of physiology, can be the greatest times for the greatest climbs of one's life.

That year, like every year, we held Creeksgiving, our annual Thanksgiving celebration at Indian Creek. The modern incarnation of Creeksgiving, our version at least, began out of necessity; it was raining, and we were bored. When *Alpinist* had me write an article about it, this was how I described the birth of our Creeksgiving:

An acid test of sorts for the climbing community, this non-event was born of friends gathering for Thanksgiving weekend at the Super Bowl campsite in the early 2000s. There was a man they called The Mayor, a stubble-faced sage who took care of everyone with a shyly welcoming grin.

One year, it rains as it never does in the desert: continuously, filling up long-forgotten washes and ensuring that the Wingate sandstone is soaked for days.

Sure, we could start drinking, but instead we stage a 4K footrace around the campground. I pull a variety of costumes out of a duffel bag. Our friend Shaun works for an athletic company, and he produces a bag of socks and hats. That night, we have a dance-off. People wrestle in the mud—grown men driven to madness by rain and alcohol, writhing on the desert floor.

And that was how it began. It was overwhelmingly male, and drunken. The dance-off was just me and Mark. It ended when I tried to jump over him and ended up kicking him in the neck. For a moment, I thought I'd paralyzed one of my best friends. Mostly what I remember from that first year was being wet and how much fun that little footrace around camp was.

The next year, that glorious desert sunshine returned. Women showed up. The dance-off was crazy. Many participants. Costumes. A half marathon, running out to the South Six Shooter from camp, jumaring up it, and then running back. More traditions came about, but the most impressive was the thankful circle. For a moment in time, the partying stopped and everyone got quiet and still. Each and every one of us said what we were thankful for. The themes were always something about nature and our community. It was never money, dominance, or success. I don't know if the word *utopia* is fitting, but in those moments, faces lit by a massive fire, stars beaming above in the stillness of a desert November night, I knew our culture was onto something.

That was the foundation of what built up to this Creeksgiving. For the starting line at the races, Shaun had constructed a structure he dubbed Adam's Arch, with prayer flags flying in the breeze. From the right angle, the arch framed the North Six Shooter, giving it a sacred feel. This celebration had a sacred feel. Adam loved Creeksgiving, especially the half marathon we named The Turkey Shooter. He called it America's Greatest Footrace.

That year, the turnout went from thirty or forty of us to over a hundred. I never felt like it was too many. I wanted this event to be the gathering of the dirtbags, where we meet one last and final time for the year and share drink, food, and ideas. Meeting new friends and sharing seemed to be the ultimate way to end the climbing year. The more you climb, the more you realize that climbers are some of the greatest people on the planet.

The food table was as long as Incredible Hand Crack, with a queue to match. The Mayor had cooked several turkeys in fire pits all day, tending to them while everyone else was out running, climbing, or on vision quests. He didn't say much, but everyone knew he was The Man, the guy in charge without ever saying he was. That's a leader for you.

Tim was the other leader—the host of the campfire games and, of course, the thankful circle. He was sober now too, and a much better host, I should add, after he made the switch from beer to soda for his nightly beverage. And we made a better DJ team too, for the dance-off, now that he was sober.

That night we danced wildly, until the wee hours of the morning, giving thanks to life, and acting wild, not the reckless abandon of binge drinking, but rather celebrating the divine beast within, and sharing everything with our people, our culture.

The next morning was the hangover, which is never much of a problem in the desert. It's not like you have to get up and go to the office and hide your shame of a night spent going too big. You move slowly in the morning, maybe hit the peace pipe for some relief, get your coffee going, and then eat a big breakfast. That usually takes care of the hangover. This hangover was one for the event. Some bystanders, part of it but not fully invested, said there were too many people. Too loud. I thought we'd come there to party, to celebrate. We always meticulously cleaned up after ourselves following these events, leaving the site pretty much the same, if not better than before. That said, we listened to their complaints.

The following spring came the final blow—at Creekster, a little knock-off celebration held over Easter weekend. Just as we were about to have a big dance-off, we caught the police spying on us. We felt like teenagers, but with the repose of being adults. We just went over to the cops, to where they were hiding in the bushes, and asked if we could help them. They told us they were there for our own safety. We knew they expected someone to smoke some weed, and they would step in and write a massive ticket, as the fine for marijuana in Utah is over one thousand dollars. Instead, we smoked no weed and held a silent mustache competition. Even the applause was done silently. Rumor has it, back at the station, one of the cops said to their sergeant, "Well, we didn't bust them for anything. They were actually very quiet and apparently have a thing for mustaches. Any other leads for us, Sarge?"

And that was the end of our Creeksgiving in Super Bowl. We moved our celebration to a more low-key campsite and toned down on the partying. Not necessarily because we almost got busted, but because we were all toning it down on the partying. Shortly after, a new type of human being started appearing at our celebrations, babies. Plus, when it comes down to it, we go to the desert for one pursuit above everything else, the climbing.

For years, I'd been driven to get high on big walls. It was where my heroes tread, and it was where the purity of climbing exists. Those experiences, half a mile above the floor of the earth, led to the greatest revelations, highs, visions, and clarity of mind.

After El Capitan, my desire for wall climbing diminished. Perhaps it was growing older, or perhaps it was just my surroundings. The Black Canyon was no longer an hour away. Yosemite was no longer in my waking dreams every day. Durango was so close to the desert, and thus the desert became all that mattered to me in climbing. Just like wall climbing, the desert is a fantastic rabbit hole to go down.

I started to view the desert in a multitude of ways. As a home. As a canvas to paint my art. My own field of dreams where I could return to a childlike state of being, with the hindsight of an adult. A place where I could progress my vision of what it meant to be an American climber.

I started to visit Indian Creek in each and every season and learned her moods and her colors. I watched and studied the crowds. Some days I was simply part of that crowd, just another climber lining up at the base of a splitter crack, waiting to test my mettle. I camped with my friends, new and old, in numbers oftentimes large, huddled around a massive fire. The hoards of people, rather the hoards of us, we were (are) predictable. Busy in the primetime of spring and fall, the numbers swelled larger and larger every season. The parking lots, by force of automobile, or by paving from the government, got larger and larger.

Other times, like in early summer, you could have this entire place to yourself, or so it seemed. A place is not a place that can be home to a young man unless he has made love in that place. In my younger dirtbag days, the desert would always magnify my loneliness. There were always so many more dudes around than ladies, and that started to change in the climbing world, right around this new decade. And that was okay then, for it is good for a young man to be lonely when he is alone, the true crime is being lonely and being surrounded by so many people, the way a human is lonely in a city.

So where I once prayed to the stars for the simple comfort of a woman, ten years later, moving as stars and dreams often do, everything was answered and given. In Super Bowl, where we once had massive epic parties over Thanksgiving, in the summer the land was back to quiet and uncrowded. My new lover and I could walk around naked if we wanted to and would not be noticed. It was so hot that you did perhaps want to be naked, but this is the desert—it's not always romantic, the reality of bug bites and other venomous creatures usually took away the notion of this place being a romantic paradise. In the summertime, the snakes, scorpions, and spiders outnumber the climbers you'll see. When I found my stride again, making love in a tent, while the heavens erupted into a magnificent thunderstorm, there was a feeling of belonging, a feeling that I was home.

On trips like these, in the so-called off-season, conditions were far from ideal for climbing, so we hiked and explored the land. I realized in my fifteen years climbing there, I'd overlooked so much, or maybe this place just needed that long to feel comfortable with me, and for me to feel comfortable with it. One day while hiking, we stumbled upon massive petroglyphs, twenty feet tall and fifteen feet off the ground. Some looked like deer and elk, others hunters, and some appeared to be beings from another planet. I could hardly wrap my mind around their massive size and how and why the artist created them. Was it the beauty of the desert that drove her or him to create these works of art that outlasted the people living here? Or was it boredom? Or was it something as big as an alien life-form visiting, and they had to share their message? None of these questions were answered.

The more we went down the rabbit hole, the more we found. The irony of Indian Creek is that, while certain areas are crowded, there is still a vast landscape of buttresses to explore, and new routes abound. Even when the rabbit hole led to buttresses that weren't any good for climbing, there was still this sense of adventure that we were visiting places that had hardly ever seen a visit from a human being.

With all this newness and openness in the air, the search for new routes began. It started simply enough; we began carrying drills in our packs to fix up old anchors and make them safe for ourselves and the general public; the nature of the sandstone in Indian Creek is delicate, to say the least. Then we would see a line, around a bend, the ridge, just out of plain sight, that appeared as though it had never been climbed. We already had the drill up there, so we'd arm ourselves with it and the necessary tools and do battle until the crack was a climb.

This process got addictive, and on every rest day, I'd find myself hiking new cliffs. Most of the time the hikes led to nothing more than a good view. One day, Tim joined me on a hike, and we found a slab that looked like a meteor had struck it, like a basketball sized rock from space crashed right there, leaving a crater in the slab. We shook our heads in amazement.

That day, we drove way up a canyon no climber really ever drives up and hiked up a wash no one ever hikes up. After an hour and a half of trudging, sweating, and cursing, we got to the rock where we hoped to find our new dream wall. Tim was as hooked on the experience as I was and never flinched when I suggested these hikes, which usually were just dead ends in the rabbit hole. This buttress we found, that day, was the absolute worst section of rock either of us had laid our eyes upon in the Creek. We hiked alongside it for what seemed like hours, no signs of weaknesses in the rock in the form of cracks, the only way to climb in the Creek. The sun turned the corner onto this west-facing cliff in the afternoon, and we sweated and cursed some more at our lack of luck. But we kept hiking. Then we found something.

As a writer, when I've interviewed people, it's like you're always trying to coax something out of them. I've noticed something though, often at the end of an interview, when I put the pen down, and we're just talking, that's when they say the most profound, articulate things. Like, for my lack of trying, but just sitting there listening, that's when the magic happens, and on that day, when Tim and I gave up, we found our holy grail.

We turned the corner, baking in the sun, dehydrated, feeling we were on a quest with no ending, cotton mouthed and spaced out, and came across a perfect splitter crack that looked like it arched leftward to the heavens for a couple hundred feet. Then we found a cave, and there were many cracks in it. Most importantly we didn't see any evidence of human activity—this was a cliff that the birds still owned. We walked down the wall, and everything was there that a good Indian Creek wall needs to be classic: good hangouts, cracks right next to one another, and a killer view.

Then we found another cave. It was trippy. Of all the walls in Indian Creek, only one has a route in a cave, the aptly name Cave Route on the Battle of the Bulge buttress. For us, it was like we'd discovered gold. Climber's gold.

Both of the caves we found were bigger than the one at Battle of the Bulge. This second one we came across refracted the craziest light, a purple hue with an aura that it was neither day nor night; instead of dark and intimidating, this little cave was welcoming. Once we stepped out of the cave, we were reminded of our surroundings again. The view was a new one for us at the Creek—to the southwest, the southern edge of Canyonlands unfolded, a tight maze of canyons, white-capped sandstone fins, needles, and mini towers. Abbey country. Then there were the ever-proud Six Shooter towers, the South Six Shooter where we run to every Thanksgiving, short and stout, the most popular and easiest tower climb in this corridor. Then the North Six Shooter, standing taller, prouder, like the older brother, protecting the region, a monument to the absurd, acquired beauty of this desert, and there was much in between, with a blue sky overhead.

The discovery had been made, but there would be little instant gratification. We began an hour-and-half-long stumble back, down loose gullies, through chinle layers that feel like your walking on ball bearings; a busted ankle out here would mean a long involved rescue. We hiked and hiked and lost our excitement for our discovery because we were fatigued, and then we got lost and couldn't find the car, but, just as the sun was going down, we realized we'd overshot it, and Tim's old Toyota truck appeared out of nowhere. We hopped in, I cracked a beer, Tim a soda, and we toasted to more days out here, on the edge of the Indian Creek corridor.

This was late spring, and we knew the wall would have to wait until the fall. Even when the fall arrived, there was unfinished business for other new projects. I had been obsessively trying a thin crack climb I'd established a couple years before. For me and this rig, it was like an abusive relationship. At first I thought I'd never be able to do it. The beginning is so small you could barely fit a ruler into the crack. Somehow there are face holds out right in a dihedral and weaknesses in the line for your feet. Those moves alone took me several tries to figure out. Then the crack widens up for the tip of my pinky and there are a couple of moves like that, right foot desperately stemming out, and conditioning the fingers to love the pain. Finally the crack gets really steep, and the clock-is-ticking, this-is-a-fight type climbing starts. The crack becomes more offset, and thus you can't even put the edges of your toes in it like you normally would. The finger jams get better, but this is where I would always fall; I didn't have the strength to pull through. Season after season, I tried these moves, probably thirty attempts over the last couple years, and with each failure, I felt about 49 percent frustrated and 51 percent committed. I had to finish the business.

In October, with Tim belaying me, I finally got it done. All the practicing, all the rehearsal led up to sending the climb, and in the process, I realized what giving a climb your all truly meant. All these years, I was an imposter if I said I was really trying my hardest, but I knew I had more to give.

With this project wrapped up, and some other less memorable ones finished as well, we set our eyes on the Cave Wall. The cool thing about developing a new wall is the adventure and the variety. Not every day are you in the mood to try hard; sometimes it's just the art of climbing, the friendships, and the surroundings that matter.

Tim and I were raving to everyone that would listen about our new discovery. Half of our friends were interested; the others knew the manual labor involved in developing a new wall and had no interest in climbing new cracks when there were so many classic ones already developed. But, just because a library is full of books doesn't mean you shouldn't try to write your own.

The first day up to the Cave Wall, I rallied my new friend Hilary. We'd only climbed together once before, but she was keen on the notion of hiking for hours and scoping new lines. Her dog, Scout, a charming mutt with perky ears and hints of golden retriever and Australian Shepard, was even psyched. So we drove out the long wash on a hot early autumn day and hiked for almost two hours, scrambling over loose terrain and following the accompanying doubts that come with the adventure of newness.

All of a sudden, we weren't in the Indian Creek I knew well anymore—this was the Wild West again. From our vantage point, you couldn't see the highway, and no cars drove out the wash we drove up and started hiking from. This was solitude, and I didn't know Hilary that well. I didn't have the luxury of having a partner that I knew inside and out.

We arrived at the base of the wall, awash in sweat, and Hilary still seemed upbeat. I was impressed. She'd passed the first test. I gave her a tour of the wall, like a proud new homeowner. But, I didn't own this land, and hopefully no one ever would; things like this should always be shared.

Everything was fresh, and loose blocks were everywhere. On our hike circumnavigating the wall, I stood on a block the size of a refrigerator, and it just started moving down the hillside. Terrified, I just rode it for a couple feet, until it promptly stopped. There are moments in climbing experiences where you feel brave, almost fearless—this day was not one of those moments. This was humble pie for breakfast, lunch, and dinner. No cherry on top for dessert either. This was the virgin desert.

We were in my desert home, but everything was so different.

Looking out to the Six Shooter towers, we didn't see anything other than the landscape, not even a car drove out there the entire day. We had somehow, someway found ourselves in part of Indian Creek that belonged to the past. I guess that's why they should call climbing a pastime; we're always trying to find a forgotten magic, a field of dreams of sorts.

We had so many new climbs to choose from. Dihedrals that soared as far as the eye could see, big headwall splitter cracks, offwidths, and shorty lines that were obvious, low-hanging fruit. Being in a new place with a new climbing partner, we both decided on the easiest possible line, a sixty-foot crack that looked like it had perfect hand jams the entire way.

We exploded our gear at the base. I armed myself like always, a fat rack of cams and a haul line I'd use once I got to the stance where the anchor would be drilled. Then Hilary would send up the drill kit, and the line would become a climb. The climbing of the crack was luckily very straightforward, and just as I suspected, it was perfect hand jams. The crack ended, and I plugged a bunch of cams in, anchored myself to them, and had Hilary send up the drill kit. I drilled a bolt, and then started digging in the bag for the blow tube, to clean out all the rock dust from the hole, so the bolt could safely be pounded in. The tube was nowhere to be seen. I looked in every little compartment, nothing. I looked again. Nothing. I cursed, but not the type of yelling I would have done if I were up there with one of my bros. There was a woman down below that hardly knew me—I had to at least try to keep it together. *The Cave Wall is not off to a good start*, I thought to myself.

Then Hilary shouted up, "What about the tube from your hydration bladder?"

Brilliant. She looked at my hydration bladder, and somehow, luckily, the tube that connected to the bladder easily came off. She tied it on to the haul line, and I dragged it up. It worked! I cleaned the hole, pounded in the bolt, and then repeated. We had our first route at the Cave Wall. After that one, we did another short crack line, a productive day.

As the sun started to slip away, the magic hour of golden light descended. The way it reflects on the crimson sandstone walls is always cause to pause for a minute and reflect. But as the sun descended, so would we, stumbling down the hillside, trying to pick the line that someday would be the trail and avoiding the steep, dangerous terrain to skirt down the hillside safely.

That night we ended up at Super Bowl. Like always, friends new and old shared food and fire—it was still the good old days. In the morning, when the sun came back around, I could see the wall back in that forgotten canyon, way off in the distance, sitting there right in plain view of where I'd spent many of my nights and mornings.

Obsession began. Other than sex, shelter, and food, the Cave Wall was all that mattered. I preached to my friends, and luckily, like always, they rallied. One by one, everyone approved. The approach was a bitch, they agreed, but it was worth it. Each time we hiked up and down, we found a better way too. The drive and the approach were the blessing because they guarded the cliff. To the hardcore, leave-no-trace-type environmentalist, leaving the land untouched entirely would be the ideal scenario. Not us, we'd rather use the public land, and let it settle into our souls, you know, become one with it, all that bullshit. And then, after our little footsteps left a trail and we had enough climbs, we'd share it with the community—don't keep it a secret: this land is your land; this land is my land. Woody Guthrie style.

All seasons must end. However, the way autumn slips into winter in the desert is precarious and never predictable. So, in December, after the first storm, the weather report indicated decent climbing weather, and we formed a posse and rolled out.

During the fall, we were able to establish these magnificent climbs. Works of art they were. Nature started, and we added the necessary human touches. I'd found a new personal project that was truly art. Again, like my other project, it started tiny, ruler width, and then opened up to a massive headwall with a crack just over an inch wide. I knew to successfully climb this crack would mean I'd have to become a disciple of the wall, that it would work me, over and over, and that I wanted it to punish me, because in the end, something great would come out of it: a first ascent, but more importantly, I would become a stronger, humbler climber.

Gene had his eyes on this dihedral that went so far into the sky you couldn't really see the end while standing on the ground. We'd stared at it many times, and Gene decided that day would be the day. It was magnificent, and when he reached the anchors, we all agreed it was the longest continuous single-pitch dihedral we'd ever seen. Gene, who is reticent to name a climb before it has been free climbed, couldn't help himself, and suggested, "What about To The Moon?"

Ah, and there it was. We were in the middle of developing a wall we knew would be our finest contribution to the climbing world; it was simply too good to think we could find any better. We were okay with that. At some point in life, you have to take a step back and realize this is your moment in time, and it might not get any better. The thing with our sport is that it is not the climb that matters the most, it is the climbing that matters the most. Sometimes the climb is so good, the companionship and camaraderie so right, you've got to ride the adventure all the way, all the way to the moon.

Chapter 35

Last year during the winter holiday season, while flying back home from Illinois, I was in Phoenix for a layover. It hit me that, since my trying times as a twenty-year-old, when I was hanging on to life by a thread, I hadn't returned to that place because, after all, there was no reason to. I didn't give it much thought, until the flight took off and I looked out the window to the hills and surrounding mountains. Somewhere below me was that hill I climbed, where I found the courage to reach out to my parents and end my life as a runaway.

These days, I can hardly believe I reached such a level of depression. It's not uncommon to read about a young person taking their own life—it's too commonplace. Just the other day, here in Durango, a young man took his life. When I read about a suicide, I always think of my own time with those thoughts, and I get sad, even if I never met them, that they couldn't find their way from the darkness back to the light. I also realized I was just going through my journey when I lived in darkness for so long. It was no one's fault that it happened, other than my own. Again, like climbing, experience is only gained through experiences, and like Martin Luther King Jr. said, I am grateful that I have seen the mountaintop.

That vantage, that little place in my mind, keeps me going. Like everyone, I have my ups and my downs. Lovers have come and gone; I fall in and out of love. My aspirations in life are minimal: I want to write, to eat, to climb, and to make love in tents. When I'm gone, scatter my ashes in that Colorado Plateau desert that has given me hope.

Just a couple weeks ago, I was heading out to a local climbing area, driving up with my buddy Jon. We talked about current affairs, about politics, and the state of the world. I lamented about some of the things I wish I were doing better in my life. A relationship had just ended with a woman I loved. My bank account was hovering near zero. I was wondering if I should have taken another path, if I should have stayed with the security of the job I left behind long ago.

He just looked at me knowingly and said, "You have freedom—at least you still have freedom."

Check out more of Mehall's writing at:

www.climbingzine.com

lukemehall.blogspot.com

About the author

Luke Mehall lives in Durango, Colorado. He is the publisher of *The Climbing Zine*, an independent print publication and website, and he is the author of *The Great American Dirtbags* and *Climbing Out of Bed*. He is a proud graduate of Western State Colorado University in Gunnison. He enjoys climbing, sleeping in tents, hip-hop, yoga, and uninterrupted mornings of writing. Luke loves hearing from readers and can be contacted at luke@climbingzine.com.

Made in the USA
San Bernardino, CA
19 May 2016